To
Janet, Paul
michele & Ellen Burkett
with every Good
wish & Prayer that
Joy & Peace may come to
you out of every conflict
you face! may you see
Beyond Trouble to the Good God sends!

E. Leonard Dillinger

Dealing with Conflict

E. Leonard Gillingham

Abingdon
Nashville

DEALING WITH CONFLICT

Copyright © 1982 by Abingdon

Library of Congress Cataloging in Publication Data

GILLINGHAM, E. LEONARD, 1931-
Dealing with conflict.
1. Methodist Church—Sermons. 2. Sermons, American.
I. Title. II. Title: Conflict.
BX8333.G48D4   252'.076   81-20662
                                     AACR2

ISBN 0-687-10329-0

MANUFACTURED BY THE PARTHENON PRESS AT NASHVILLE, TENNESSEE, UNITED STATES OF AMERICA

To

my wife Martha
and our children
David, Mary Len, Carol, and Sara
whose love and devotion
have made beautiful harmony
out of life's tensions and conflicts

ACKNOWLEDGMENTS

Life's greatest joys have come to me because of those who introduced me to Jesus Christ. His attractiveness was first reflected to me through my parents, who seemingly never wavered from love, truth, and loyalty, no matter how intense the conflicts became. That beauty was further magnified through the people of a little rural church in Oklahoma, Highland Methodist Church, where radiant joy was seen as patient, accepting love.

After I left home the universal love of Christ became more evident through people of the churches in which I participated. Over and over these devoted pilgrims of faith gave unmerited kindnesses and demonstrated through their own tragedies and conflicts the important healing power of truth and love. As their pastor I shared the intimate secrets of their souls; from that sacred privilege, my life has been nourished with the goodness of God.

I am indebted to B. C. Goodwin, whose longtime friendship and inspiring faith persuaded me to accept this challenge, as well as to the Joint Communications Committee of The United Methodist Church for the invitation to preach for the 1982 United Methodist Series of the Protestant Hour.

I will be forever indebted to Dr. Hugh Halverstadt, Professor of Ministry at McCormick Seminary, whose genuineness and creative insights focused my attention on the importance of skills in conflict management. He has been the key person in shaping my thinking about conflict management theory and application.

As soon as the invitation came, I received numerous calls and letters from friends, many of whom described the inspiration that would come from David Abernathy, executive director and producer of the Protestant Hour. Dr. Abernathy's life, insights, encouragement, and tireless effort to assist me in this project were inspiring and personally enriching.

I am also grateful to the staff and to numerous members of First United Methodist Church of Albuquerque, New Mexico, who have read and typed this manuscript and have assumed additional duties so that this series of sermons could be developed.

CONTENTS

INTRODUCTION

Conflict exists universally. It can neither be avoided nor ignored. Whether it creeps into our lives or hurls itself at us with hurricane force, conflict must be dealt with. Conflict comes when two or more values, procedures, feelings, or interests collide or are in discord. It can be internal or external, intense or slight, but its presence diminishes our happiness and has the potential of destroying us.

Few issues deserve more urgent attention than conflict. As a pastor for thirty years, I have seen many lives wrecked by poor conflict management: powerful people crush the weak, fearful persons capitulate to the bully, angry individuals rebel with terrorism, timid ones withdraw in despair, while others escape into fantasy worlds—tranquilizing themselves with drugs or tinkering with their emotional machinery trying to adjust to their dark nights of desperation. Poorly managed conflict has drenched our world in the blood of our wars and made the United States groan under violence six times worse than that of any other industrialized nation. It has caused some of our institutions to become "junk piles" of broken lives and left us with emotionally burned-out people while our world teeters on the brink of annihilation.

Although I am a person of hope, our human management practices are cause for alarm. The daily news reports that powerful groups are locked in mortal combat with each other, economic forces compete for control, and we lack any referees who can demand that we all live by some common rules of human decency. When it comes to where we live and work, conflict occupies a major amount of time. Conflicts threaten our homes, our communities, our churches, and our own sanity. The ethic of "might makes right" is altogether too common for comfort.

The military is so mechanized today that many soldiers hardly realize that war is about killing people. One mother told me how startled she was that her son wanted to make a career of the military service. She was even more amazed that he thought war was flying airplanes, managing electronic materials, and playing hospital. When she asked him if he thought he could be happy with killing people, he answered, "Of course not." "What do you think war is about?" she asked. He had no reply. Shooting guns has been so sanitized it seems very far removed from death. As a pastor to the nearby Cannon Air Force Base in Clovis, New Mexico, I discovered that pilots were so busy flying planes and doing their assigned jobs that there was almost no personal connection with the devastation they were inflicting on human beings.

The art of warfare that separates the killer from the killed makes mechanized annihilation simple and painless. "Out of sight, out of mind." Insensitive persons who do not reflect on the result of poorly managed conflict can bring about mass destruction, as Hitler did in the Holocaust.

Where can persons find guidance in handling conflict, strength to cope with the emotions it generates, or the courage to attempt creative solutions? In my struggles I found little help in Christian circles—very few books, courses, or informed people—but I have found a sturdy faith.

While flying to Kansas City, I joined in conversation with a world traveler from New York. The talk soon got around to the condition of New York City and the world. Curiously I asked, "Do you think there is any hope for the world?" He paused in his rapid talk for a moment and said hesitantly, "Yes, but I don't know why!"

Listening to his response, I became aware that biblical faith rests deep in the hearts of people. For in the Bible are found clear traces of how people of faith handled some of the most intense conflicts the world has known. The Bible grew out of conflict. Both Judaism and Christianity searched for eternal values while they fought for survival in the Fertile Crescent, where the crosscurrents of Eastern business and culture marched through their borders. The Judeo-Christian legacy endured the conflict of powers, struggled with decisions that offered life or threatened death, and left light on the pathway for those who walk through an imperfect world. The Bible also reveals how the grace of God, seen in mighty and wonderful acts, has established victorious people who are hopeful and joyful.

Biblical wisdom is relevant for us. It is marked by candid facing of reality; it offers criteria for decision making; resources for coping with the perverseness and frailty of humanity, and an ample historic record of lives transformed. It tells of blind people who get vision, the dead who find life, and the angry who find love. Its pages tell of evil's disregard for others' dignity and how this is exposed and thwarted through the crucifixion and resurrection of Christ, which empowers us by the most powerful symbol of hope the world has ever known. We need to feel that power today.

Timid people may shrink from conflict, but Christians are called to confront it; not with absolute answers—that would be idolatry or heresy—but with the creative love seen in Jesus Christ. That requires health and skills for living. This world often disregards others and discounts love as a viable criterion for decision making in the marketplace. The steady call of Christ brings us back again and again to get involved, to develop and demonstrate skills that restore harmony, balance, and peace to the world.

The world was created by a loving God, who did not mean for it to be destroyed. God did not intend it to be a pile of broken lives, paralyzed people, or a battlefield where people destroy one another. Absolutely not. This world was meant for harmony. It was created that way, and God is active in restoring that balance and harmony.

God's will has been made flesh in Jesus. God's spirit has been poured upon all creation. The breath of this Spirit sustains us, keeps the world in balance, works for good in all things, and calls upon us to respond in faith and love. God is still active today, guiding us through the treacherous conflicts that threaten to destroy individuals and community. God restores broken relationships, forgives sins, heals the wounded, and makes all things new. This ruling activity of God is good news because it calls upon the world to recognize and follow a course of conflict resolution that leads to a richer and better life.

CHAPTER I

MANAGING
YOUR CONFLICTS

One of my earliest lessons in managing conflict took place on our farm in Oklahoma. It occurred one spring when two beautiful black colts were born. We named them Dan and Dolly. Raising horses was not just a convenience, because where we lived farm work was still being done by horse: mowing hay, plowing, cultivating the fields, pulling the wagons, and riding the range. The addition of these new colts would soon make possible the expansion of the farm since I was getting old enough to manage part of the farm work myself.

These two colts came into the world playful and fascinating. They grew quickly, and soon we noticed the difference in their personalities. They were like two children from the same family. What one liked, the other hated. Dan was gentle and curious. Dolly was wild and suspicious. Dan was submissive, Dolly was rebellious. Dan quickly conformed to our human ways; Dolly rebelled against every hint of them. These animals soon began to represent life to me. In

Dan I saw a loving, affectionate, and playful spirit. He noticed every noise and movement as if it were something good about to happen: something to eat or something to enjoy. On some of those dew-drenched mornings on the creek banks, he would follow my brothers and me, eager for our gentle caressing. We loved what he did, and he loved what we did. The world was a big, friendly place for Dan.

We began preparing him to fulfill his role on the farm: pulling wagons and plows and running at a gallop through the pasture with one of us on his back. We petted him and lay on him. Finally we put one of my younger brothers on his back and introduced him to a halter and then a bridle. He accepted the role easily.

Dolly was a different story. For some reason, she was suspicious of people. When we came out of the barn she would throw up her head and run away, eyeing us as if we were enemies. We offered her ears of corn and even sugar cubes, but she would stand off and wait until we left before she would eat. We liked to pet Dan's silky nose and loved his affection. We wanted the same from Dolly, but she would bite or kick us if we did not pay attention.

One morning Dad said, "It's now time that we start training these horses for the work they must do." Though I was not there, I heard the stories of how quickly Dan accepted the new role and how bitterly and long Dolly fought against it.

Dolly represented for me the negative extreme of life. Some people rebel against everything, create trouble for everyone, reject all affection and love, and operate with a negative, independent spirit, conforming to nothing. Their spirits are nasty. They are a pain to themselves and others.

On the farm, our effort at managing the conflict between the needs for horsepower and the wills of the horses to be free and independent also raised for me the purpose of the human being on the earth. Were we really meant to have "dominion" on the earth and create order here? Back then the answers were simple: Dad said so, and that settled it.

Within each of us and within each community there is that independent drive to do as we please, as well as the desire to cooperate. Each of us finds people who are suspicious, negative, and distant, as well as those who are curious, amiable, and easy to work with. We also search for our roles on this earth and seek to know how to relate to others with whom we often have conflict.

The development of the Hebrew people, recorded in the book of Exodus, is a fascinating study about the conflicts experienced in forming a nation. It tells about a group of wandering nomads who become slaves in Egypt but escaped and formed the nation of Israel out of their learnings in the wilderness. The chief leader was Moses, whose clever mother devised a way for him to gain the wisdom of the Pharaoh's court while she taught him the dreams of the Hebrew people found in Abraham.

One day he exploded in anger and killed an Egyptian for unjustly flogging a fellow Hebrew. As a fugitive Moses escaped to the mountains. Forty years in the mountains could not erase the dreams given to Moses nor the cruelty of slavery etched in his mind. The burning bush became a holy place for him, because there he had made a full commitment to do God's will.

Moses' task of rescuing slaves from their masters proved to be difficult. The Hebrew people had to be motivated, educated, and united about the potential of God's will for freedom. The Pharaoh had to be convinced that it was God's will, or at least in the Pharaoh's best interest, to let the slaves go. Proposals and counterproposals were made. Agreements were made and broken. Finally, with the promise that there would be no more suffering and death for the Egyptians, Moses left Egypt with a joyful group of ex-slaves.

In conflict, fear and pressure made people change their minds. Moses had hardly got to the Red Sea before the Egyptian heads of state had reversed their decision. They were fearful that the economy would collapse—who would do the dirty work of society? So the Pharaoh dispatched the military to capture and bring back the fleeing Hebrews.

When this news reached the camp of Moses, some of the ex-slaves, who had lived by fear, began to panic. They feared reprisals and death. They complained about the foolishness of leaving and Moses' crazy dream. All of them were aware that the sea blocked their movement and they knew that Pharaoh was pursuing them. They were trapped! Even Moses had no viable solution.

Then Moses made a strong statement of faith: "Fear not, stand firm, and see the salvation of the Lord, which he will work for you today." That did not seem a very tangible alternative, but it was all they had at that moment.

The Lord's answer seemed harsh and incredible. "Why do you cry to me? Tell the people of Israel to go forward!" "Go forward," God says. It is your only hope.

Moses commanded and the Hebrew people

marched through the sea on dry land, but the Egyptians perished in the waters as they tried to follow. That miraculous event is celebrated by the freedom-loving people of faith to this day. These ex-slaves had no expertise, no equipment, no knowledge of how to run a government, and certainly no skill in handling the conflicts between a pursuing army and a big sea. All they had was a faith in God and a willingness to go forward—walk in and through their conflicts.

When you walk by faith you see only the horizon—you do not know what is beyond. For Moses the sea was only the beginning of the conflicts created by "going forward." It was God's will to move forward; but in the wilderness life's necessities had to be provided—food, water, health care, and protection from disease. Furthermore there had to be rules of behavior for these nomads and ways to enforce them. Moses' inability to handle all the disputes alone required the creation of an elaborate organization. The religious needs of the people had to be met. He had positive and negative people. All had to learn discipline. In fact, Moses had to provide for the total well-being of all of these people. To go forward meant to handle every problem as it arose.

Moses was called to manage conflict. He had never done it before: he didn't know how, he didn't like it, but it was necessary before the dream of freedom could be a reality. His training and preparation had helped him learn how to accept criticism, consider impossible odds, keep his wits about him, and not panic when the going was tough. He no doubt drew upon his own past experience, using the knowledge gained in Pharaoh's court and utilizing other existing codes of behavior.

There were other times when Moses did not know what to do: all he could do was say, "Trust God." Some challenged his leadership and even revolted. Grumbling was common. The negative, pessimistic attitudes of these ex-slaves kept them in the wilderness an extra forty years. Their independent, uncooperative, undisciplined lives multiplied the conflicts Moses faced; but he and they were trying to move forward as God directed them. The Ten Commandments made the requirements of restraint clear, and other laws sought to deal with human conflict justly. Moving forward meant taking all conflicts seriously.

All groups must deal with the same kinds of issues that Moses experienced or that I had at my home on the farm. Whether a family, a church, or a government, all groups must deal with order and conflict.

There is an interesting similarity between the creation of Israel, described in the Bible, and the formation of the United States. This became clear to me when I was memorizing the Preamble to the Constitution of the United States. "We the people of the United States, in order to form a more perfect Union, establish justice, insure domestic tranquility, provide for the common defense, promote the general welfare, and secure the blessings of liberty to ourselves and our posterity, do ordain and establish this Constitution for the United States of America." Our leaders were seeking guidelines for the resolution of conflict so they could live in peace and provide protection for the whole nation.

The story of Moses graphically displays how the children of Israel responded to discipline. There had to be order, but it came slowly. Adjusting to their roles and limitations in the society created conflict, but it also saved them. Everyone could not be in a place of authority; yet everyone in the society needed to have a place of importance and have some influence in what was going on.

Moving forward for Israel meant learning their purpose on earth—to be God's people, living by law. They learned fair play as they sought to interpret the law and restricted their retribution to no more than "an eye for an eye." They shared a common goal and dream. As they faced their problems they had to develop a faith to see the future and the discipline necessary to achieve what they dreamed. They saw all of this as God's gift to them.

When I was a young manager on the farm, I began to think about God's struggle with the world. We are placed on this earth with a special role and we are expected to fulfill that role. Sometimes we accept it lovingly and easily, but at other times we fight it intensely.

We all live in conflict. Each of us has a free spirit and refuses conformity, but we also face the necessity of living in community. Each of us has a different idea of what our role should be; therefore relationships are always in conflict. Some of us fight the pressure to conform and hate the conflict it generates. We can refuse to join civilization and be like our wild horse Dolly and the Israelites who challenged Moses' leadership.

On the other hand, we can be placid, docile, and accommodating to everyone in the world. We can try to do everything, to be everything; but then we will find ourselves slaves of the system, like our horse Dan. Some people like that are victimized by every wind that blows. They have not established any identity and have not yet grown to see their own worth. They grumble to themselves about others and about their situation in life. They have never dared to express themselves. They are like the chaff that the winds blow around. They are like Dan and those who preferred to be slaves in Egypt.

Most conflicts arise over who we are in relationship to all the others. The role we are going to fulfill troubles us. Dan and Dolly were brought into the world for a purpose by the farm managers. We are brought into the world, Genesis says, to have dominion over the earth, to replenish it, to subdue it and "to till it and keep it." Our role on the earth is not always one that we like. Sometimes we grow into the role like Dan—accepting it, learning it, warming to it, and it seems natural. Sometimes we are like Dolly; we fight it, rebel against it, and resist it all the way.

It is possible to find a middle ground, where we meet in a circle of friendship, united by our common faith in Christ. In that kind of community we all seriously ask ourselves about the purpose of God. We also look at the faith and love by which Jesus lived and see in him the ethic for our relationships. Relationships create conflicts, but love calls us to manage them by a mutual determination to find a constructive way to live in the world.

President Lyndon B. Johnson said, "A president's hardest task is not to do what is right but to know what is right." Finding that right balance is the hardest task for all human beings, who, in one way or another, are managers of conflict.

I still remember my father's interpretation to me on the farm. "Len, we all have a responsibility to manage this world for the Lord in a constructive way. I believe

God has given us that role, and we need to learn it wisely—that's why we have to train these horses to help us." Training those horses meant both creating and managing conflict on the farm.

Moses saw a distortion of God's intent for the Hebrew people. They were not meant to be slaves, and Moses saw himself in conflict over their treatment. He wanted change, but the task seemed impossible. His only criterion for attempting this task was his confidence that God did not want them in slavery. That conception was rejected by the Egyptian people in power, who fought and resisted. It took time to determine that freedom has the blessing of eternity. The new Israel discovered that freedom could not be absolute, it required restraint, cooperation, and a system of conflict resolution.

Living in relationship to any other human being requires conflict management skills. Moses found that communities must develop working agreements. They must have a common respect for each other and a desire to manage conflict constructively rather than arbitrarily or capriciously. Sometimes Moses felt the solutions were not present at all. At first he lacked the organization to get things done. Later he did not have the confidence of the people, but the early instructions from the Lord gave him the chief approach to manage conflict: the Lord said, "Moses, go forward." That is the only way out of the problem. Go forward. Attempt the impossible. Discover solutions no one else has found. Find the wisdom of God in community and in relating. Listen to the conflicts and search for the creative answers. God calls us forward and promises to be with us, as we use the best wisdom available to us.

In society, as on the farm, conflicts do and will exist. As managers, we are charged with the responsibility of working with God to bring order out of chaos. We are to responsibly seek for the balance God intended. We are to strive for harmony, not disharmony; work for solution, not destruction; establish good will, not broken relationships. We are all called to manage conflict. It is up to us to become more responsible and skilled in this task.

CHAPTER II

WE HAVE
TO MAKE CHOICES

Growing up, for me, was a painful process. There were many conflicts, many people to answer to, and many answers to find. It seemed that life required me to do something with myself, but how was I to find out what? That puzzled me, even at an early age.

When I was ten years old, my friends and I created a system of collecting soft-drink bottle caps. Underneath some of the corks were messages or prizes to prompt us to buy a certain brand of soda pop. But somehow we began prizing the bottle caps themselves. Not only did this venture provide the city with a scavenger crew of boys who picked up old bottle caps, it also created among us boys a society of values. We came to give real worth to those caps, trading them to one another for comic books or candy bars.

My bottle cap collection was enormous because I had the advantage of a paper route, and this led me to places where bottle caps would be discarded—service stations, recreation centers, and restaurants. Within about six months, I was able to collect well over ten thousand. That meant I was one of the wealthiest boys in the city, and it gave me power over the other guys. It meant I could control their behavior to a certain extent, and I could also determine the worth of certain kinds of bottle caps. Accumulating these caps paid dividends in my own feeling of accomplishment. I had demonstrated to myself that I could discipline myself, make decisions, and manage my affairs.

Our gang spirit created a system of values that were as real as any adult system. When others attempted to steal my bottle caps, I became possessive and put locks on the garage doors to protect my investment of time and energy. When someone was caught stealing caps, we all were quick to give a corporate reprimand. By then I had learned that stealing was wrong, and my sense of indignation at those who did not share that value system was extremely intense—they were not playing fair and were threatening to make our whole community collapse.

But those great days were interrupted! It came when someone told us that the bottle caps had no intrinsic worth of their own. I remember when we talked about that among ourselves. We denied the truth of those thoughts and said, "They don't know what they are talking about." The grief work started. Then most decisions were easy, but when the values for which we had lived were discovered to be worthless, it was a painful process to leave the past and move on. We were being accused of giving more value to these bottle caps than they deserved. We had given our time and energy in collecting them, storing them, and protecting them. I was angry that anyone could tell us that what we were doing was worthless now. It was several weeks before we were willing to acknowledge that in the real world of adults, bottle caps did not buy anything. We instinctively knew that, but we were having so much fun living in our own fantasy world we acted as if this were not true.

The day came that I accepted that reality, however. The old system had broken down—the bottle caps could no longer be traded. Younger kids didn't have that value system, adults didn't have that value system, and even our own group no longer considered the caps of value. The night was a long one when I faced this reality and made my peace. I had to change. Those bottle caps had to go. I had been a wealthy youth, but my real value was no longer measured by bottle caps. Sitting alone, I made the decision. In the morning, I would get the boxes of caps, stacked neatly in hundreds, take them to the trash can, and dispose of them.

After finishing breakfast and taking out the trash, I went to the garage, got those cherished boxes of caps and nostalgically took them to the trash can. I listened to the sound as I dumped them in. I remembered the good times, the feelings of power and worth. Those memories would remain. When I finished, I looked in and wondered what the trash man would think when he saw a barrel filled with bottle caps. Would he laugh? Or would he understand that a young boy lived here who was learning about life—a boy who was growing into manhood, learning values, and trying to find the way forward? I did not have time to reflect very long before Mother called with another task. So I turned from the past to move into that strange and uncharted future where every growing person must walk.

Now that I am older, I look back at this childhood event and can hear the Apostle Paul talking to some new Christians about the same problem. "When I was a child, I spoke like a child, I thought like a child, I reasoned like a child; when I became a man, I gave up childish ways" (I Corinthians 13:11). The Christians in Corinth were in mortal battle about who were "real Christians" and who were not. They were arguing among themselves about whether it was more righteous to be a follower of Peter, Paul, or Apollos. They were trying to decide what to brag about to one another—which is a way of trying to determine what's important. They were also trying to formulate a pattern of relating to one another when they had conflict. Likewise they were trying to determine what discipline was required of the Christian community—could you do just anything and be considered Christian?

Paul recognized the struggle of the Corinthians. They had grown up with a certain value system, a way of relating, a lenient moral ethic, and general disregard for how their actions affect others. Since they had become Christians, they were giving up an old, familiar pattern for one that was considered better. They did not know how to work through the difficulties. This all came to a climax for Paul when the Corinthians began to fight over speaking in tongues. Those who spoke in tongues tended to feel that this gift was superior to other abilities—such as teaching, giving, helping, healing, and analyzing what was going on in the world. It was to this group that Paul wrote appealing to them to reconsider their values.

His proposal for solving the conflicts of these Christians was so powerful it has become known as the love chapter in the Bible—I Corinthians 13. Paul said, Let me show you the best way to live. Then he argued that love supersedes our ability to do everything. If there is no love, productivity, talent, and skill are as worthless as bottle caps. He then indicated how love operates. It moves in stages, just as people move from childhood into maturity: "When I was a child I spoke, I thought, I reasoned like a child; when I became a man, I gave up childish ways."

Paul wrote to the Corinthians from the perspective of years. He was preaching in Ephesus when he heard about the conflicts at Corinth that were threatening to splinter the church and destroy the reputation of Christianity. As he addressed their current problem, he looked no doubt at his own development. Paul could not forget his growing years in Tarsus and his commitment to be the best man he could be. His idealism had led him to become a rabbi who would teach others. His zeal got him the finest education available. His experience with the hedonism and immorality of the gentile world made the disciplined righteousness of Judaism's laws attractive. His youthful dreams to keep himself holy were clear. His values determined his use of time and energy. When he saw the new group of Christians threatening the laws of Judaism, he fought vigorously to eliminate that distortion of the truth. But the day came when Paul had to face a new reality. There was a depth of value in Jesus Christ that he had not anticipated, and this made all his old values like "rubbish."

As Paul reflected on his own experience he described the insights he had learned over the years. Conversion had not solved all Paul's conflicts. "Look," he is saying; "life is a series of stages we go through: when we were children we thought as children, when we were adolescents we acted as adolescents. Young adults strive to become independent. In our middle years the responsibility shifts again so that, with more perspective, we begin to make our own decisions. As mature adults we rethink our relationships to our parents, decide about life's future, adjust to our limitations and mortality, and try to make the best contribution we can, since our years are limited. The next stage is old age, which requires us to examine the whole philosophy of life and decide what to pass on to others. At this stage grandparents pass on clear and simple summaries to their grandchildren. Then comes the final stage, and the preparation for it—death. So the stages of life consist of a series of adjustments and choices."

Most of us need assistance in adjusting to the new roles required by the new stages in our development. For most people becoming a grandparent is an eagerly awaited event. My wife could hardly wait for our children to get married and have children. She makes a vocation of being a parent and grandparent, but that is not the case for me. I heard the announcement that we would be grandparents. I understood that our daughter would have a baby and that Martha would go to be with them. I would have to keep house alone. Frankly, the reality of being a grandparent was hard to accept. I still pictured myself as a young adult. I was busy with my life, the church, the community. Time had gone by so fast I hardly knew I was getting older, and now I was about to assume a new role. The passage into this stage of life was thrust upon me by all the other grand-parents who began to remind me about grandparent-hood. They asked, "How does it feel to be a grandparent?" It must have taken a thousand of these questions to convince me that I had to make this adjustment. That continued for about six months; then suddenly it stopped. Somehow they sensed I had accepted it. I had entered another stage of life, assumed a new identity, and was learning to celebrate it. I think this is what Paul is trying to say to us. As new requirements or opportunities present themselves we have the option of denying them, hiding from them, avoiding them, or growing to meet them. We can fight over them or we can accept them as the God-given stations celebrating the new realities we discover.

My experience with the bottle caps, and Paul's experience in Judaism, both serve as a lesson. All our experiences become the raw material from which we can gain perspective for living. Our experiences with older friends and with younger acquaintances provide us with important insights. But those insights will be missed if we are too busy with our own "bottle caps." Love is the key that gives perspective to all of life. It must supersede money, status, or power.

There is no instant maturity for anyone. Everyone struggles to master each new stage of life. With new stages come new anxieties and new challenges. That is the way we grow. Who is the fully mature person? At one time I looked at my thirty-year-old dad and thought he was mature. Now, as he nears the age of seventy-two, he has a maturity I never dreamed possible.

In fact, life is not so much an achievement as it is a pilgrimage. We are always in transition from what was to what will be. It is a constant and consistent moving toward that shore from which we all put out to sea. All the studies of science, anthropology, and sacred history confirm this reality about the processes of life.

Life is a series of choices. Most of us create our fantasy systems and imagine that these are of ultimate importance. Sometimes we make our gold and wealth of such importance that we spend all our lives stacking it up in banks and securities, as I did with my bottle caps. Then one day the real value is exposed, and it does not meet the deepest needs of life. Sometimes we pursue the game of being important. We fight for status and recognition, looking for the limelight, and we want others to praise us for what we have done. Sometimes we like the power of status and the ability to control others with our wisdom. But then the deeper needs of the soul surface, and all the value we gave to power and status vanishes like evaporating fog before the rising sun.

Sometimes people reach in despair for any value that lasts; and they stand at the trash cans of life, where they have thrown their life's collections, their energy, and their loves, and mourn. They continue in anger because of the loss, for they would like for life to leave their fantasies alone. But life makes its demands as we confront new stages, requiring us to decide how we will accept them.

Paul called upon the early Corinthian church to grow up. He calls us to give up the childish ways of early stages—to learn from them and move on into the future. The chief choice we have is to accept the love that God offers in each new movement of life. All the knowledge, status, and achievement of life is transitory. It is only a tool by which love can be shared. Love is the food of the soul which keeps us strong through the various stages of our lives.

We have the capacity of holding on to our bottle caps, of course, and we can demand that they be accepted in life as having absolute value. Or we can give them up and accept new values. It is like the process of death. We can either grieve over what we lost or rejoice over what we have enjoyed for so long, then move on with confidence to the next stage in our growth.

For better or for worse, this world rests upon the individuals and groups who recognize and accept the hard but glorious fact that we are responsible for our choices. Life soon forces us to recognize that we fabricate systems of values and status that do not satisfy or endure. Nevertheless, they are the systems by which we operate until we can find a better way. We can choose to make our systems absolute, or we can recognize their limitations and laugh at ourselves and our beautiful, elaborate "bottle cap collections." Then we can choose to move on to the new responsibly, sharing with others what we have discovered.

Surely God is calling our world to grow up beyond the stage of "bottle cap" mentality. With this new perception, we can see that many people are still struggling to give up lesser values for greater ones. Sometime we all struggle to find the faith by which we can admit that our lives are collapsing so we can move on to the new stages of life. God calls us forward by choice. We can decide to leave the more childish ways to accept the world of surprises which comes ever fresh with the new developments in life. We handle this conflict by choosing to affirm the value of growth as God's gift.

God is the giver of every new creation. By faith we can learn to live with enjoyment in the present and accept the reality of the changes that life brings. After the process of grief in giving up some things we cherish, we can move on to embrace and celebrate the new gifts of God, as the caterpillar accepts its new life as a butterfly.

CHAPTER III

IMPOSSIBLE EXPECTATIONS

I had gone to bed and had just moved into that first level of deep sleep when the telephone rang. I fumbled around for the phone, only to discover that the call was from the director of the International Hot Air Balloon Festival being held in Albuquerque. Patiently I listened as her story unfolded, trying to get my mind focused on what was going on. Then it became clear. Two balloonists had been killed in a tragic flight across the 10,500 foot Sandia Mountains just east of the city. The pilots were anxious, wondering whether to continue with the races. To help calm everyone, the festival committee wanted me to conduct a memorial service at the launch site at 5:00 A.M. Would I do it?

Now, I don't have instant memorial services for balloonists stored in my computer—almost no one is ever killed ballooning. Yet I had become the unofficial chaplain for many of the balloonists, and I love the sport myself. I wanted to say yes, but I feared to—what would I say or do? I wanted to say no—but I recognized that the community expected me to assist them when they had serious problems dealing with fear and death. They were reluctant to ask me to do this at such a late hour, but their sense of desperation dared them to try. By sheer faith and confidence in the power of the gospel, I decided to conduct the memorial service.

Sooner or later everyone is asked to do what seems impossible. When I think of the demands placed on managers, physicians, public servants, teachers, parents, blue-collar workers, and those who hold two jobs, I wonder how they do all that is expected of them. The expectations seem to be impossible.

Not only are the expectations tough in the work force, they are also tough in the home. Husbands expect wives to be good looking, good cooks, and good mistresses without any hassle. Wives expect husbands to be considerate, good providers, and supportive. Who has found the perfect spouse? Is it fair to expect any relationship to be perfect? Don't impossible expectations destroy relationships?

There is a passage of scripture in the book of Acts that deserves some attention. It describes how two disciples faced an impossible request. Shortly after the violent crucifixion, the resurrection, and Pentecost, the disciples were sent to teach and make disciples of a very hostile world. Despite rejection by the leaders in power, Peter and John were going to the temple at the hour of prayer. As they approached they saw a man being carried to the place where he daily begged for alms in front of the temple. When he saw Peter and John, he asked for alms. Peter looked directly at him and said, "Look at us." There was a pause; no doubt it was obvious that they had little money, but the man expected them to give him something anyway. As their eyes met, Peter said, "I have no silver and gold, but I

give you what I have; in the name of Jesus Christ of
Nazareth, walk" (Acts 3:1-8). And they took him by the
hand, lifted him up, and he began to walk; and he
entered the temple with them.

The Christian faith is sensitive to the needs of people
to find health and renewal. This scripture passage in
Acts describes a highly motivated set of disciples
commanded to take the gospel to the whole world.
Surely that seemed an incredible task. Furthermore
they were surrounded with the many cries of hurting
people wanting the help they had come to expect from
Jesus' disciples. As religious people the disciples were
vulnerable to the demands of others because of their
sensitivity and care for people. Soon, people made
impossible demands upon the disciples. They expected help, perfection, and sainthood.

The beggar at the gate knew that Judaism demanded
its members to give to the poor. He saw his chance to
ask for alms. He did not want a fortune; he just wanted
a meal and a place to stay. As Luke portrays these
leading disciples facing the impossible expectation of
this beggar, he highlights their wisdom and compassion. They look at him, listen to his request, and
respond.

The location of my church in downtown Albuquerque puts me into contact every week with many
transient people who want and need help. They ask for
it and many times demand that I give them what they
want. Furthermore, if I help one today, I know that
tomorrow I will have another ten to help. The requests
are impossible. The needy know that our religion
teaches us to give, so they seemingly take advantage of
our consciences. There was a time that if I did not help
them all, I felt guilty. I thought I must do everything for
everyone.

I have wondered what Peter and John felt as they were approached. Maybe they were so full of the spirit of Christ that they could look into the eyes of that beggar; but most of the time, when we see a person who we know is going to ask for help, we make sure that our eyes don't meet. There is something about eye contact that hooks us.

Our world suffers from many pains. If we look into the eyes of people around the world we know the needs are incredible. We especially pay attention to the physical ones, but we are now beginning to understand the emotional ones and are also stretching to grasp the spiritual ones. Healers are needed. The writer of Acts recognized that, but he also captured a very important message for people of a new age. Listen to Peter's words to the person who expected help from him, "I have no silver and gold, but what I have, I give you."

The lessons in those few words are many. It may seem intuitively obvious, but we cannot give what we don't have, any more than we can come back from where we haven't been. That is the injunction all through much of the Bible. You are not to love others instead of yourself, but as yourself. We are to love as we have been loved. You are not to negate yourself and neglect your own needs.

When people come to us expecting the impossible, we need to know and declare what we don't have. Peter recognized his limitations. He didn't borrow money for the beggar, nor did he feel that he owed the beggar a living. There is a limit to what we can do for others. We need to recognize our limits and say what they are.

If we could learn that first lesson there would be fewer burned-out, cynical people. Today's society places a lot of pressure on public-interest groups. Everyone wants everything. Furthermore, servants of society often lack that clear, crisp vision by which they can judge their accomplishments. When goals are not completely clear, external forces begin to set your agenda and you relinquish your ability to control your own life. Unclear goals become the means by which we become slaves to others.

When we have to make decisions about the demands placed on us, we must deal with our own wants and desires. As I dealt with my late-night telephone call, there were many conflicting desires going on inside my mind: the desires to please a friend, to fulfill my role as minister, and to be recognized in the community. On the other hand, there was the impossible timetable: there was no time to prepare and almost no knowledge about the situation. The long hours of work the day before had already taken their toll on my body. I was also tired of the multitude of requests that I had been handling. I had a fear that I would bring discredit to the ministry no matter what I did. If I didn't go, it would be a rejection of the balloonists. If I did a poor job, it would humiliate me and my ministry. Many of us often face these conflicting desires and do not know what to do.

As if the problems accompanying excessive demands are not severe enough, there are always false prophets who stand around and give poison platitudes to conscientious people. Can you imagine the insensitivity that advises them to "stick in there," or "when the going gets tough, the tough get going." Those macho comments are a throwback to the occasional crisis day when a little encouragement would provide that extra ounce of effort. They were not meant for the highly motivated, dependable, reliable persons who give 100 percent of themselves consistently to unending and impossible requests for help.

As Peter faced his request, he declared what he could not do. There was a wisdom in that no. Peter accepted his limitations and communicated them.

Sometimes we expect impossible things of others too. Our unrealistic demands create unnecessary conflict. In one of my first counseling cases as a minister, the fellow's first words to me were, "I'm going to get a divorce!" "What's wrong?" I blurted out. "She doesn't love me anymore," was his reply. Not sure what to say next, I asked, "What makes you think she doesn't love you?" (My observations suggested that she did.) "When I wake up in the morning she doesn't have her arms wrapped around me anymore," he said. "How long have you been married?" I pushed. "Almost a year," he answered. For me, that expectation seemed impossible. But for him, he believed it was required. That story was matched a few years later by a wife who expected her husband to send her greeting cards—in her mind that act was the evidence of love. But she never told him her expectation; instead, she expected him to know intuitively what to do to make her feel loved.

When we fail to communicate our own identity to our spouse, our friends, our peer group, we may lead them to expect more than we can really offer. We need to share our skills, hopes, dreams, and limitations. Our failure to be clear guarantees misunderstanding, pain, rejection, emotional trauma, and maybe even burn-out.

Our world faces many conflicts. The presence of crime, war, and terrorism all beg for solutions. There is much despair and unyielding bitterness. The stakes are high, and every effort must be extended to resolve these conflicts. But despite the needs, there is a limit to what we can do. We don't like that reality; it's hard to know where our limits are. But the management style of living expected by God is that we give only according to our capacity—we are to give our best.

If we could learn to give only what we have, we would learn first to say no, and then a qualified yes. When persons are trapped by the fear of saying no they are not ready for the serious problems in today's world. God expected us to be "in charge" of (to have dominion over) ourselves and the choices we make.

Peter was not acting alone. He had the other disciples as close friends. He had received generous help from Jesus and knew how Jesus had handled his limitations too. His experiences had demonstrated that when Jesus was tired he would go to the mountains or get into a boat to gain some privacy for a while. It surprises me how many times I read the Bible and miss these passages. Jesus grew tired and had to rest. He said no to people. In the health of that group, Peter also learned to say no. Sometimes we assume that people in a common task find support, but that is not always the case. Often the intensity of the workplace, the task, and the problems at hand provide no time for personal support building. Trying to do impossible tasks without support is to guarantee failure.

Healthy living requires a good support group. If you are going to attempt the difficult tasks in the world, you need good friends who will be candid and caring. We cannot live without love; furthermore we cannot see ourselves without honest feedback. These disciples had a close band of people with whom they could talk about the most intimate details of their lives. That provided the insight they needed for healthy living. It does for us too.

Often we attempt to do impossible things simply because they need to be done and because we love people. That is all right as long as we take time for ourselves and our own needs, acknowledging and accepting our limitations. We have to accept our limitations and our humanness in order to prevent burn-out.

One day while I was donating blood at the blood services center one of the nurses began talking about the demands sometimes placed on them. She said: "When we run out of blood, some people fly into a rage as if it were our fault. We try to explain that we can only give what is given to us, but that doesn't satisfy them. Then we argue that they have no right to think that 5 percent of the population who give blood can supply it for everyone. Even that statement doesn't work. The time finally comes when we accept their rage, tell them we are sorry, and recognize that they are making impossible demands."

Because of our limitations, we must plan to be most effective. Many of us in the Christian faith avoid planning, preferring to be "led by the Spirit." If we were to read the scriptures more carefully, we would discover that God gives great attention to planning. The picture of Jesus in the Gospels demonstrates that Jesus had a clear plan of action. He was in charge of his life, and everyone knew that. Peter and John were part of that plan. "You give what you can."

Stress management skills also need to be developed. Where social pressure is intense, we must find ways to identify quickly our own stress and to reduce its impact. It helps to monitor our emotions regularly, talk about our feelings, and maintain a good balance between work, rest, and recreation. Prayer and meditation can also help us gain additional insights and strength. Wise use of personal time management helps us to avoid agreeing to impossible expectations.

Cultivating spiritual health helps us be more effective in our thinking, vigorous in our efforts, and realistic in our endeavors. One friend keeps telling me, "The hurrier I go, the behinder I get, so I take time to keep my spirit healthy." Spiritual health helps us keep our purpose and vision for living clear. It links us with enormous resources and helps us accept and cope with failure, sadness, and death. Spiritual health keeps us hopeful in the present and in the future because we know God holds the future.

The wisdom of Peter in his statement to the lame man—"I give you what I can"—was important for him and for us. We do what we can, joyfully, acknowledging what we cannot do. Work is not everything in life; life is everything. Money is not the most valuable thing we have to offer others; love is. Yeats advised us not to search all through life for the perfection of work, but rather for the perfection of life.

Life is full of impossible demands. Sometimes these demands come from within, sometimes from without. Conscientious, hard-working people must especially beware. Since we are not all-powerful we are forced to decide what we shall do. The salvation of the world is not up to us—that is God's work. Our part is to be faithful. By this code of behavior we may attempt the impossible, but we will avoid the burn-out that so haunts today's world. We cannot give what we do not have, but we can share what God has given us. We can be like Peter and acknowledge what cannot be done, then reply: "But what I have, I give you."

CHAPTER IV

HANDLING REJECTION

The novel *The Cracker Factory* by Joyce Roberta-Burditt describes a very intense scene where Cassie is confronted by her husband. Cassie drinks too much and is an emotional wreck. As she begins to talk to her husband about herself, he flies into a rage and races from the room, shouting at her across his shoulder, "Cassie, you're a loser," then slams the door behind him.

The rejection carried in the words "you're a loser!" is magnified through the eyes, the shouts, the slammed door, and the intense motions of Cassie's husband. The opinion of no one else seems to matter to her. She feels judged, condemned, and doomed forever. His statement was a bomb that destroyed her feeling of self-worth.

You have probably had similar episodes when you felt rejected by some person significant to you. This feeling of rejection may have occurred because you were not chosen in a sports event or because you did not get a raise or promotion or because your spouse left you or your friends abandoned you. You may have seen the look of rejection in the eyes of others and thought, If looks could kill I'd be dead.

There are also times when the experience is more than just a rejection of your ideas, values, and thoughts. There are occasions, like the one in Cassie's life, when you are rejected as a person. When that happens your whole existence is questioned, and powerful emotions begin to work.

Rejection of another's ideas, thoughts, or contributions is common. Conflict arises because life is composed of a series of choices. When you embrace one value, you reject another. When you establish one set of goals, you give up others. "You cannot serve two masters," Jesus said long ago. "You will love one and hate the other."

The first response to rejection is anxiety. Rejection threatens your worth, your value, your very existence. If rejection comes from a person of significance and power or if the rejection is emotional, the trauma is even more intense. You become nervous and uncertain. Your mind races with fear as you consider possible courses of action, and you get defensive.

As a radical form of rejection, the Hebrews put criminals outside the gate where they were cut off from association with other persons. Today, teachers sometimes put children outside the classroom door, and parents punish children by sending them to their room. Sometimes people are placed in institutions. Regardless of the form, rejection uses fear as the means of motivating a person to make changes. Rejection is felt as demand and pressure limiting freedom and independence.

Rejection is a form of death. Since life is relational, the withdrawal from a relationship is a temporary

death. Jesus observed "that every one who is angry
with his brother shall be liable to judgment" (Matthew
5:22). Broken relationships, whether they were ended
by anger or self-righteous rejection, isolate us; and
isolation leads to death. The anxiety resulting from
rejection is like the anxiety that comes when we face
death.

The second response one can make is to reject the
person who rejects you. When threatened, threaten
back—an eye for an eye, a tooth for a tooth. Don't let
others destroy you, for that would be suicide. "Only
the strong survive," we say. You have power and
should exercise it. Rejection can be a two-way street.
The husband argues that if Cassie is not healthy
enough to live up to the marriage expectations, if she is
going to be sick, then the obvious response is for him
to reject her.

According to anthropologist Jean Pierre Hallet, the
"basic urge in life is survival." Acceptance seems to us
to be essential for living. We must find some place to
win. But since that is impossible all of the time, we
must learn how to survive. In high school, my coach
reminded us frequently, "Only one team wins at the
state tournament." The coach meant that most people
in the tournament were going to be losers.

Life demands that we deal with the problem of
losing. In fact, consistent winning is achieved by only a
few people. There is only one president, one
corporation head, and one winner in each of the
Olympic contests. But the temptation is always the
same—when we lose we blame others, criticize their
judgment, or assume we were framed. It is another
way of rejecting those who rejected us.

The third response is to turn the experience inward.
Those who do this begin to tell themselves that they

are worthless and deserve the rejection. When they hurt they withdraw like the turtle. If the issue is not faced it may affect behavior and personality for years. Like Cassie, we give a lot of authority to others. We believe that other people know our actual worth. We allow them to assign us to hell.

I have noticed that people are more convinced by critical remarks than they are by complimentary ones. Sometimes we will not believe a compliment unless the person also criticizes us. It may take ten compliments to equal one act of criticism. Our need for support multiplies when we are rejected. We retreat inward, hide from others, and drop out of relationships. If this continues, we are soon faced with a feeling of hopelessness.

When I headed the Office of Equal Opportunity community action projects in Clovis, New Mexico, I discovered that 70 percent of the dropouts in the schools had been isolated by students and sometimes by faculty members. They did not participate in sports, the arts, or interest groups. Furthermore, these were the persons who generally made no contribution to the community. In time we discovered that many also became criminals. They acted out the anger they felt about being rejected. Rejection was a source of community problems, arising from emotions turned inward.

The fourth response to rejection is to run—to escape through sickness, alcohol or other drugs, or through some obsession. Sometimes we cannot handle the anger or the hurt and the only way we know to avoid our memories of rejection is to escape. We try to build a fantasy world which shuts out the pain that torments us in those quiet moments of the soul.

The fifth response is to take a balanced look at life.

All of us are realistic enough to know some losses are normal. Rejection is bound to occur. We normally learn very early in life that there is a difference between losing and being a loser. Losing is a normal reality of life, but being a loser is an attitude that causes us to give up in despair and hopelessness. Realistically we know we can expect to win sometimes and lose sometimes.

Most of us look for a better way to handle the losses and the rejections which come to us. Rejection demands attention. Failure to handle it leads to retaliation or withdrawal and finally to dropping out. Running leads to living in a make-believe world. Persons need a healthier way of managing the conflict found in rejection.

I suppose there has been no harsher experience of rejection than that which came to Jesus of Nazareth. The story really begins when Jesus determined that he must make some ultimate choices about his goals and priorities in life. When he was baptized by John the Baptist he announced to the world that he was making an absolute commitment of faith to the kingdom of God and would demonstrate this faith by his love for all people.

Jesus' self-understanding was clarified even more as he wandered those forty days in the wilderness and on the Mount of Temptation. From that mountain he could look below and see the Qumran center—a community of political and religious refugees who expected God to intervene and solve their problems. Across the river he could see the land of Moab, and his imagination could sweep him to the Sinai, where the children of Israel had their dreams of a Promised Land flowing with milk and honey. Just below him was the city of Jericho, where Joshua first entered Canaan.

He no doubt recalled all the futile efforts of living for

bread alone and those who had appealed to the people through the use of the spectacular. He recognized the historical efforts to control everything through economic, political, and military means. With all the options before him, he decided the direction of his life—Worship the Lord only and demonstrate that in all his daily affairs.

That decision brought immediate conflict in Nazareth, so he departed for a place more accepting of him—Galilee. From Galilee he launched his effort to proclaim the presence of God's kingly rule in the world. He declared to people paralyzed by sin that they were forgiven, demonstrating to all the world that God's mercy and kindness are for everyone, they are not just the exclusive privilege of the few. This campaign constituted rejection of the tradition so cherished by Judaism. Jesus' values were seen as a rejection of the Jewish laws, which had become ends in themselves instead of means to help people. The laws had become absolutized.

At first Jesus' ministry was novel and attracted attention. With time its implications became obvious to the leadership of the nation who saw in him the ideas which would change the whole society. At first they thought they could handle the conflict by ignoring it or posing questions to Jesus. Failing at this, they resorted to intense techniques of intimidation, pressure, and rejection.

We read that "the high priest tore his robes, and said, 'He has uttered blasphemy'" (Matthew 26:65). We hear how the crowds united with the authorities; we get the picture of the powerful forces gathered for Jesus' mock trial. Pilate has his authority from Rome. The religious and political leaders of Israel claim authority from Moses. The crowds emotionally shout their anger—release a criminal, but crucify Jesus. Their rejection was intense.

Notice now the way Jesus experienced rejection. In the early part of Passover, Jesus was heralded by a crowd. As the week wore on, Jesus was feeling the pressure and reached out for support from his closest and most trusted disciples. He agonized over his impending death, no doubt questioning whether he had done all he should and wondering if it was worth it. As the tensions grew, more support vanished. As the threat of death became clear, one disciple denied him and another betrayed him. The rest ran to hide. Jesus was left alone for the trial and for the crucifixion.

Jews were repulsed by the act of crucifixion. The fact that this was directed toward Jesus indicated what a heinous criminal they considered him. He was accused of being a traitor, a blasphemer of their God, and one who dared to criticize the sacredness of their absolute law. We surely understand this action, because today people who are traitors to our laws are destroyed and those who do not conform are ridiculed.

The next scene revealing the aloneness Jesus experienced in rejection is that of his death. His mother was there feeling all the agony of death as well as the shame people had heaped upon her son. Maybe she felt a little blame or helpless anger at the cruelty of the world. By her presence she was affirming him in his last hours and sharing the shame which people said he deserved. He could see her from the cross, knowing that she also suffered from the goals, priorities, and values for which he lived. In his death he must also bear the agony of watching his mother suffer for his commitment.

Reviewing this sad scene in human history gives us some clues about our own handling of rejection. It is inspiring to see great people, for they seem to handle things so gracefully. But sometimes we fail to understand that they have the same frailties which we have. Jesus deserved more attention in his handling of life's issues than he was generally given. By stressing his divinity and denying his humanity we miss what God revealed to us in him.

Jesus' presence in Jerusalem was not an accident. God had a plan, and Jesus had a plan. He set his face with determination to go to Jerusalem to plead his cause. He was not blind to what he faced. But if he was to change the world, if he was to guarantee that all people had the right to God's love, he had to confront the center of power with his conviction. If people rejected him, that was a risk he had to take! His convictions were more important than life itself.

The second observation about Jesus is the clearness of his purpose in life. He acted wih focus and clarity. He knew his identity and affirmed it. In fact he felt his identity was affirmed by God. That spiritual reality gave him a sense of unequaled self-worth. Jesus did not make the mistake of getting his sense of self-worth from people, as Cassie did. He found it in God.

The third claim of Jesus was that no codes, laws, or persons were absolute or infallible. God was not just a historic reality. He was not some distant deity but a presence with us now whom he called by the intimate term "Father." Jesus, too, lived by faith in God.

We would omit a very important part of this story if we ignored Jesus' emotions as he dealt with the agony of rejection. Anxiety drove him to prayer. He gathered his friends with him and went to the garden of Gethsemane. In prayer he could once again get his purpose clear, face the emotional turmoil, plead his case before God, and renew his confidence in God's faithfulness. He was looking not for magic, but for confirmation.

In anxiety he reached out to his friends, but his friends could not handle the pressure of this rejection or they failed to understand the serious threat that he was facing. Often our friends do not hear or understand us, even though they try. Sometimes we doubt that anyone can fully understand our pain.

Jesus' story highlights for us the power of an eternal view. He had already recognized that choices have consequences. It is difficult to do anything without a trade-off. His style of life was to get his priorities right and trust the consequences to the test of time and the grace of God. Jesus looked through the rejection and trusted his offering of love to the goodness of God. Sometimes there is no other way. God alone is the final judge of life. There is more to living than others' approval.

The story of Jesus' rejection was transformed with time. The human race did not have the last word. What the world thought was so absolute and infallible proved to be relative and fallible. Sometimes the only solution to rejection is the lonely and solemn test of eternity. When tensions rise, you humbly offer the best you know, tested with all the wisdom you can glean, then wait for God's decision.

God had the last word about Jesus' rejection. And this confidence now cheers the whole of the Christian faith. God can be trusted. The kingdom of God does exist in the midst of the world. God's mercy is present, and the Holy Spirit does guide us. God had the final word to the world. God had the last word about the cross. This event transformed the massive act of rejection by an eternal affirmation that brings people all over the world to their knees in reverence and inspiration two thousand years later.

We all have rejection in this world. But no affirmation is greater than the voice of the eternal God saying, "Well done, good and faithful servant" (Matthew 25:21). Is any judgment worse than the rejection of history and eternity? Those who rejected Jesus were rejected by history, while Jesus, who was rejected, has become the Savior for millions of us today. God's involvement in history affirmed the faith and love of Jesus. Truly, in this world, all of us lose once in a while, but that doesn't make us losers. Thanks be to God.

CHAPTER V

WHEN INTENTIONS
ARE MISUNDERSTOOD

Most of us at one time or another have been the new kid on the block—new in an organization or new to a community. As a result, we know a lot about the excitement and trauma of changes as well as the adjustments that have to be made when we make a major change in our lives.

When I was eleven years old and my self-awareness was just developing, my family moved from Taloga to Hobart, Oklahoma, a county-seat town of about five thousand. Hobart was a big city to me, for I had always lived on the farm with lots of wide open spaces and only a few people with whom I had to relate. At first this big move was exciting.

My father had just been made manager of a larger office in the agricultural association that required our moving. To my parents, this change meant more salary, a chance for Dad to advance in his profession, a brick home, new status, and the advantages of city life. They carefully described these advantages to the four of us children.

The excitement of all those advantages began to wear off after the first week. There were new restrictions, no familiar surroundings to explore, and no old friends to enjoy. I wished that I could be "back home."

For many days the grief of moving was intense. I even felt anger toward my parents. After all, it had not been my choice to move but theirs. Why should I have to suffer for their decisions? The material advantages were not worth the price; I thought it and said it.

I wanted to be part of the new group of neighborhood boys, but I was rejected and shut out. "How do you get to be part of the group?" I wondered. I intended to be a part, so finally I had a confrontation with them. I tried to push my way in. They pushed back. Then we had a heated argument about who was the "best." They were willing to test me for leadership. That meant competing with the leaders in a bicycle race across six blocks of city streets. The race course was outlined, our bicycles were prepared, and we met for the big challenge. Then the race began. All of us gathered speed, the chief leader in the center of the street and the two contenders on either side. We were racing at full speed, across open streets, through stop signs, straining every muscle as if our lives depended upon the outcome.

Suddenly, without warning, the leader, who was only inches in front of me swerved sharply into my bike. We collided in a fury of churning bicycles, scrunching sounds, and agonizing pain from bruised bones and skinned elbows and knees. My opponent claimed his foot slipped off the pedal. I was angry, my bicycle was torn up, and the other leaders were embarrassed by the event. We had not settled my role in the group, and I was hurting, afraid to go back home to let my parents see what I had done to my bicycle and my clothes.

As I look back at my experience as an eleven-year-old, I now understand that being the new kid on the block can create a lot of turmoil. In this situation the needs, hopes, and dreams of mine, my parents, and the kids in the neighborhood were in conflict. All of us were forced to deal with the conflicts my presence presented.

Our entry into every new group can produce a whole set of new conflicts to be resolved. We must make our intentions clear and settle misunderstandings as we determine the role each of us will play in the group. If these issues are not settled, the conflict can get out of control and involve the whole community.

Misunderstanding and conflict in groups is as old as the ages. The familiar story in the Bible tells how the world misunderstood Jesus. It tells how Jesus sought to care about all people, to call everyone to whole-hearted devotion to God, and to restore the law to be a means of love instead of the end of love. As Jesus did this, "the chief priests and the scribes and the elders came to him, and they said to him 'By what authority are you doing these things, or who gave you this authority?'" (Mark 11:27-28). Jesus' intentions were in conflict with the way of life common at that time.

The scribes, chief priests, and elders, however, failed to see or agree with his intentions, making their own values and intentions absolute. They remembered that God had commanded them to be holy. Some leaders had required the Jews to break relationships with gentiles and pagans, especially during the time of Ezra and Nehemiah. The very name Pharisee meant "Those who separate themselves" and described their intense desire to be pure and holy.

Jesus sought to rescue people from injustice, forgive their sin, acknowledge the present reign of God in the world, and include all people in God's love. The leadership sought to protect and conserve the progress they had made in moral and ethnic purity. They assumed the responsibility for the community and found Jesus to be a real threat to many of their cherished values. They revealed their real concerns when they asked, "By what authority does he do these things?"

We, too, face hard questions: how do we adjust to change and at the same time preserve our sacred traditions? Who gives us authority to speak the truth and to love people who are different?

Today, as in ages gone by, changes and misunderstanding create problems for every group of people. Since our lives change so rapidly now, we have new pressures to acquire more insights and skills in dealing with the misunderstandings that multiply in our world. Acquiring the desire and skills to love people who misunderstand us and radically disagree with us is not easy. Our world calls for us to find a way or be destroyed.

Misunderstanding is normal. Each of us has a different background, environment, history, and tradition. Those unique experiences shape our thinking, establish what we value and consider normal and condition how we feel about everything. In addition, every person has a unique perception of what happens. When you multiply these differences by the number of people on the earth, it becomes obvious that we will not always understand one another. We are limited. We are not born into the world with full understanding or competent skills. Rather, we come to understand our world by bits and pieces as our experiences increase. Furthermore, every move we make demands adjustment on our part and on the part of others.

Misunderstanding arises also because of our own perverse thoughts. I had a discussion with a young scientist about genetic manipulations that can determine the sex of people. "That's scary," he said. "What makes it so scary?" I asked. "Well, people can use it for all kinds of evil purposes," he declared. "Do you know any bad intentions they have?" I asked. "No," he said, "but I can sure imagine some pretty bad stuff myself." That is part of the problem. We know our own perverseness and imagine that people with power might use their power in the way we think.

Since misunderstandings are normal, our challenge is to deal with them in a creative way. From Jesus we learn that misunderstandings do not have to destroy us, nor do we have to use them as reasons to destroy others. If we see conflict as a normal reality and not necessarily evil, it can be the very basis by which change and growth take place if we so decide.

My bicycle race produced a new self-discovery for me. This became just another step in the series of learnings for life that my parents used wisely to help me grow. As they let me talk through my own angers and frustrations, they helped me think through the intentions of those neighborhood boys and my own. This helped me learn how to handle such events with patience and insight in the future. Every new experience is an opportunity for new learnings, the development of new skills, and the chance to start developing new roles in life.

As I tried to become part of that new group, my parents, like Jesus, accepted me with all my pain. That felt good. I could not deal with the boys until my parents helped me deal with my emotions. They listened to my complaints, but they also heard my deep cry for relationship. They found out what my complaints meant to me. There was healing in their understanding. My love for them grew as they helped me struggle through these misunderstandings.

Jesus used the authority of truth and love to help people. He included them in his fellowship. When he found people who were hurting, he responded. People who were lost or rejected found in him God's love, which he said was God's gift. As they confessed their sins and needs, they were healed or grew so they could again live victoriously. It helped them to find a place where their intentions were understood, just as it helped me when my parents understood.

On the other hand, Jesus intended to confront the existing powers with the damage that their rigidity was doing to people. He sought to make the world a more humane place to live. That was the way he translated his love into deeds. Because of his efforts, he was accused of taking too much authority. That misunderstanding created some serious problems for Jesus and his followers, but it generated the tension that helped Jesus' disciples grow. As a result, it also brought about essential changes in the world.

Misunderstandings can be challenges to enlarge our perspective on life. For some of us, that means to think about other people's interests, intentions, needs, and wants. So often we think only of ourselves, our own wants and needs. All of us are part of life. All of us want to belong. If we have ever been the person on the outside, we can understand the pain and frustration that comes in all new experiences. Being aware of these problems in adjusting can give you personal insight and the opportunity to help others who are less experienced than yourself.

Many misunderstandings could be avoided if we developed some important skills in communication. Love prompts us to avoid, rather than evade, misunderstanding.

When we relocate, face a serious emotional crisis, or live in a group that habitually takes things for granted, we need the additional skills of caution, patience, and forgiveness. Those are some of the skills we can develop.

Listening skills can help us avoid some misunderstandings. We must begin with the awareness that language is a very clumsy way to communicate. We all may use the same words, but we intend different meanings. It takes time and effort to communicate, but there are some techniques, although time-consuming, that can help reduce misunderstanding. The first is to take more time to listen—listen to what is actually being said and listen to what is meant—and maybe we will hear the needs, hopes, feelings, and dreams that are being expressed. The next step is to communicate what you heard back to the speaker to check your perception. You report what you heard—not "what they said" but what you understood from what was said. You are not arguing; you are seeking understanding.

In my ministry I insist on interviewing couples before they get married, hoping to help them talk through their relationship. I ask them to describe the first thing that comes to their minds when they think of the word "security." The men immediately think of making a living and supporting a family. Most women say, "Knowing that I am loved." I ask if they can hear the difference in each other's answer, but most can't.

If they can't learn to understand each other, they will both use the word "security" but never comprehend why they don't mean the same thing. Hearing and accepting the other person's meaning is a very important skill.

We all need to do a periodic checkup on our relationships. Corporations, groups, and families need some prescribed time and place where they review what they have done and what is going on. We need a chance to evaluate what we have done, how well we did it, how we feel about relationships and what our strengths, weaknesses, hopes, and dreams are. This regular, periodic check-in with each other in an atmosphere of openness and candor can help prevent major crises later on.

Sometimes strong people with active minds and capable tongues intimidate us and make us reluctant to speak. That is when we need some help. We must work for fair play and clear hearing in these conversations. If the problems are intense, we need to work in a smaller group. We cannot solve major problems by mob action. Furthermore, relationship building is done only by people who will play fair. Love fights for fair play among all participants. If people cannot relate fairly, they need a third person with authority to help them succeed, as my parents did for me with the neighbor boys.

Not all misunderstandings are going to be resolved. Not all people will play fair, and not all people have the capacity to love. Many become impatient, and others lack the skill to understand or listen. There is no guarantee that even the most skilled persons will be understood all the time. Likewise, not everyone will agree with us always. We are all unique. While that is a beautiful fact of life, it also makes relationships difficult.

The Jewish leadership genuinely misunderstood or disagreed with Jesus. The community demanded that nonconformists like Jesus be crucified. Conformity is too big a price, Jesus insisted. The smile of God is better. While Jesus had a love big enough to include them, their narrow views provided no space for him. Jesus could not resolve the problem alone, and Pilate refused to fill his God-given responsibility of administering justice. Jesus could play fair, but there was no guarantee of fair play by others. The conflict and misunderstanding could not be resolved.

Although standing by yourself may be lonely, sometimes that is all you can do. When that time comes you must present the best of your life to the court of eternity and let the God of the ages make the ultimate decision. That was what Jesus finally did.

The pain that comes from being rejected by other people drives us toward conformity; but when it requires our souls, that is too much. When that happens, we have no choice but to stand with Martin Luther, who said, "Here I stand, I cannot do otherwise."

God created all the people of the world. Everybody is unique and special. God did not mean for us to be melted down into conformity but to form a beautiful blend where each of us makes our own unique contribution. That was the way Jesus used his authority. He recognized the worth of all persons. The scribes and Pharisees and elders used their authority to condemn others and to discard God's messenger. It was their loss, but the God of history has placed the spotlight of eternity on Jesus to show us the way of life.

We can learn from Jesus to be the person God

created each of us to be and do it with love. Jesus let the authority of love and truth stand the test of death, while weaker persons try to use their authority to demand conformity. History shows us that the way of Jesus is divine but the way of coerced conformity is demonic.

Change always brings new frustrations and new conflicts, but it also brings us new opportunities. We cannot control others' understanding of us, but we can control how we respond. We can be authentic. We can speak the truth with love. We can grow through every experience. If misunderstanding cannot be resolved this way, we can leave it in the hands of our loving God, who judges all things by eternity.

CHAPTER VI

MAKING COVENANTS
AND
LIVING IN COMMUNITY

Airline pilots are the envy of many people. They look handsome in their uniforms, intelligent as they manage the switches and lights in the cockpit, and so alert as they maneuver their multimillion-dollar planes high in the air with a priceless cargo.

Occasionally I have lunch with a commercial airline pilot, and we talk about the mystique of flying. He recalls his training in the computerized simulator and the emotional traumas associated with mastering himself and his profession. He describes to me the endless systems used to minimize mistakes and guarantee the safety of others.

It did not take me very long to realize how many people count on the qualifications of that pilot. Imagine the variety among two hundred fifty persons on a plane. There is a mother with two little children who boards first; right behind her is a quadriplegic with a briefcase in his own motorized wheelchair. Several sales persons board the plane as if they were walking down the street; then there are four children—a boy of fifteen taking care of his three small sisters, all eyeing every transaction with suspicion and awe. There is a Navajo Indian with headband in place, an Asian exchange student, and a black football player who has just completed law school. There is a new college student returning home for his first visit and grandparents who eagerly look forward to seeing their first grandson. The labor-management mediator takes his place beside a young girl traveling to flight-attendant school. Row by row, the plane fills with people from various professions, from different states in the Union, and from many countries. They are seated at random beside one another, all carrying with them secret emotions, wishes, dreams, and value. For the duration of the flight they become a community of people, dependent on the pilot's good judgment.

The pilot, along with the copilot and flight engineer, keep in constant communication with one another. They examine the flight plan, check the vectors, get weather reports, monitor the plane's functioning, and occasionally talk over the intercom to tell passengers what is taking place.

The plane will also carry other valuable cargo: thousands of pieces of mail that bring hope, new gears for machinery which will keep a factory running. A casket sits inches away from an orchid being sent to a new mother upon the arrival of her new baby. The pilot moves it all.

I marvel at the power, grace, and importance of this pilot. I admire him and envy him for what appears to be a widely respected job that takes him around the world. He is surrounded by people taking his orders. It seems that this whole community is built on him.

I ask the pilot, "How do you do it all?" He says: "I am

only a highly visible piece of the whole business. I could not even fly the plane if it were not for hundreds of support people working on the ground getting everything ready and handling the system along the way and in the cities where I land." He enumerates the complexity of the system, the stockholders, mechanics, sales force, ticket persons, cargo handlers, inspectors, instructors, managers, supervisors, clerks, bookkeepers, typists, environmental specialists, control tower operators, and so on. "The list is endless," he explains.

Little by little, it begins to unfold. All of us in that plane depend on the pilot, who is dependent upon scores of others, who in turn are dependent upon hundreds more. But something has to unite all those people. What is that secret which makes this flight function so smoothly? The cooperation is partly motivated by need, partly by profit, partly by romance. But this whole operation still needs something more to function.

My mind turns to my own profession and the theology that the Bible taught me about relating to the world. I remember the apostle Paul talking about the new style of living that Christ proposed because it merged individual freedom and corporate responsibility. Paul presents a systematic argument for the creative power of faith and ingenuity in his Letter to the Romans. He argues against the old rigidity of absolute dogmatism and descriptively advocates the excitement and joy of faith-full living. In the twelfth chapter of Romans, he admonishes his readers to give all their energy to God, because that is what constitutes spiritual worship and is the glue that holds the world together. Then he tells how each individual's dedication fits into the whole. Listen to those descriptive words: "For as in one body we have many members, and all the members do not have the same function, so we, though many, are one body in Christ, and individually members one of another" (Romans 12:4-5).

Paul is saying that life consists of many different roles. In I Corinthians 12 he carries the illustration further and talks about the unity of the various parts of the body. He likens various people to organs of the body. It takes all of them to make up the whole body. There are no unimportant parts of the body. About the time we say we do not need a tiny gland or organ or think that some part of the body is unimportant, we discover that we cannot live without it. Paul declares that we must pay attention to every part of the body for survival. What hurts one part seriously hurts the whole. If I have arthritis in my hands, I may hurt so much that I forget about everything else. To ignore chest pains may bring death.

Christ is the head of the church body, Paul says, and Christ is its controlling center. It is his directorship that gives purpose and unity to the whole. As head of the body, Christ cares about every part and keeps that vital balance so the whole body may effectively function to accomplish its purpose. Yet, without our common devotion to serve the Lord, there would be no community.

This passage makes clear to me how we live in this world. Every community is held together by agreements. The only way we can live on this earth is by our implicit agreement to work out our differences in the spirit of fair play and evenhandedness. The airline functions because of a series of systematic agreements that have been hammered out through long experience. All groups function this way, and so does the human body. The body stays together because all the parts work together, each functioning as it ought to. It is this basic harmony which God created and intends.

Though the pilot commands the airplane, he is just one part of the whole team. He may be a rugged individual, but he is also responsible to the company, to the passengers, and to those who ship their cargo by plane. Who can determine what person or group is most important? Let the controllers go on strike, and the whole business can be shut down; let the mechanics walk off the job, and nobody can fly; if the company goes bankrupt the planes are grounded. If individual members or the company disregard their covenant, the whole system will collapse with disrespect and failure.

My airline picture is just a miniature description of the global community. The truth in the airline story applies to the whole world. All parts of our world are held together by agreements and covenants. Every individual has a contribution to make and a responsibility to the whole. Each person must be able to have some influence and must share in the common goals. Every group must establish its own working arrangements and must also learn to fit into the whole of the universal purpose of the world. Our survival depends upon a general agreement to make wise covenants that respect the individual and protect the well-being of the whole.

Unhealthy organizations create problems for individuals, just as unhealthy individuals create problems for organizations. When the kidneys stop functioning, if something is not done quickly the whole body is soon going to die. When individuals and groups stop functioning, the whole earth can become sick. Nothing is more important for living upon this earth than being responsible, both as individuals and groups. Without it this world cannot survive for long.

The very nature of community throws us into conflicts. As individuals we want our independence and freedom. On the other hand, we are interrelated to others in the community, and this requires some conformity. We love it and hate it at the same time. We want freedom; yet we want someone else to take care of us. We want to trust; yet we fear. We have many contradictory desires in our relationships with others. We are reliable and also unreliable. We are skilled and unskilled. We are saints and sinners simultaneously. We want to have a place of importance, but we do not want to have to share the glory and responsibility.

Living in community gets to be very complex because most of us have multiple roles. For example I am a man, seen by my children as a father; I am seen by my wife as a companion and lover; I am regarded by my congregation as counselor, preacher, and administrator; my parents see me as a son. My identity likewise varies in every group according to that group's need and perception. My wife also fills many roles: mother, wife, daughter, purchasing agent, community worker, minister's wife, relationship expert, and so on.

Needless to say, the roles all of us fill are always open to sharp conflict. In each case, the secret of community success depends upon two things: the quality of fair play in reaching agreement and the quality of the covenants we make—the agreements, the contracts. Covenants are very specific acts of love that enable us to live together in a turbulent and dangerous world. Those agreements are no better than the dependability of the persons making them, and the breaking of agreements brings pain to the whole of the body.

Sometimes we think we can avoid dealing with certain kinds of people and create our own little isolated communities, but the price we pay for isolation is a big one. No one is an island. There are few hermits, and sooner or later we are going to pay the price of what every other inhabitant does or does not do. We are all on this big ship together. We all have to depend on one another. Management depends upon labor; yet labor needs the organization that management brings. Learning to cherish every individual as Christ did seems to be essential for living.

We must someday learn that there are no unimportant people in our world. Just as every employee of the airline is important to its functioning and every part of the body for its health, so it is with the world. The pilot, no matter how powerful, is totally dependent upon all the other parts. If those parts do not function, the pilot cannot function either. It makes no difference what the creed, race, sex, economic status, or national origins of the persons who make up that airline company. Every worker is important, not just for the airline, but for you and me as we fly and for the cargo it delivers.

Jesus' life was an argument against prejudice and condemnation of anyone. It was a clear example of individual freedom and corporate responsibility. He spoke the truth in love and created a model by which life can be lived. Everywhere he turned there were people isolated for some reason or other. The Samaritans were rejected because of a supposed intermarriage problem during the captivity. The gentiles were considered dogs or worse. The Romans were hated because of their paganism and oppression.

The Zealots were hated because of their terrorist activities. The tax collectors were hated because they made profits from their fellow citizens for the Romans. Adulterous women were stoned to death if the promiscuity was with one other than a Jew. All the other ancient enemies of Israel came in for their share of condemnation.

Jesus was against this alienation. His life was a covenant with God that all people were chosen by God to be loved. Jesus defended and gave welcome to the various rejected people of the world. His acceptance was adequate to unite them into a community, which began to develop into a special *koinonia*. This, he declared, was the desire of God for the world, and for that purpose he gave his life. He united some of these almost mortal enemies among his twelve disciples— the Zealot, the tax collector, and the foreigner. He had people of quiet disposition and those of tempestuous spirit. Jesus had a vision of the world which included the rule of God over all the world. To him it was to be one great community, united by our relationship to God. Paul carried that idea further to help us recognize that we are to function as the body of Christ and each part is important. His love included the moral and immoral, the saint and the sinner.

The covenant that held this world together for Jesus was made public in the act of baptism. John's baptism declared that God deserved to get our absolute love and loyalty and that this should be demonstrated by the way in which we related to everyone else—especially those who needed food, clothing, and so forth. When Jesus spent the time in the wilderness, he faced the common temptations of all people and had to choose the philosophy by which he would make his decisions. His decision to "worship the Lord" and "serve him only" was confirmed by the way he lived. He kept his covenant with God faithfully to the death—even death by crucifixion.

The early church continued that message and used the sacred meal of Passover, updated in our Lord's Supper, as the symbol of love every person was expected to have for others. When they shared in the meal they were making agreements with God that their very flesh and blood would be offered for the sake of the kingdom of God. It was a sacred agreement and a vital covenant. All people on this earth are God's people. Those who have made their covenants in baptism and renew it by participating in the sacred meal have made a public statement that they will work with the Lord and love all as he did. But the result is no better than the quality of the commitment that believers make. Commitment to work out relationship is the great key for living.

The great Pilot of the world cannot be effective in doing the work that needs to be done until people fulfill their contracts. Covenants require responsibility. If they are not kept, soon the glue that holds us together lets us disintegrate into chaos and confusion. As Christians, we cannot just drop out because we don't feel like keeping our agreements any more, or because the flight pattern is monotonous, or because someone else is not doing what ought to be done. My grandmother used to remind us that others' failures did not excuse us from doing our job right. "Two wrongs don't make a right," she said.

Successful living upon this planet requires the mutual good will of its residents. The mutual covenants, agreements, and vows that we make together keep us functioning. That is the way the Lord created us. If we are to fulfill our roles on earth, we must pay attention to all our support systems and truly learn to work together. Like the parts of a body or the individual roles in an airline company, we all have our place to fill.

CHAPTER VII

WHEN YOU FACE IMPOSSIBLE ODDS

Do you think it is possible for a small group of people, far away from home, living in a foreign environment, with no coaches to help them and no blueprints to guide them, to create a prosperous, smooth-operating community? Imagine this group of people in a primitive jungle. Many of the group are ex-convicts, some are religious radicals, and all are fiercely independent. How would you rate their chances of success? What kind of community do you think they might form?

That is precisely the way the United States of America began. These pioneers left many hated institutions in the old country: autocratic rulers, repressive laws, rigid community demands, and abridged freedoms. They considered freedom so important that they risked the uncharted unknown and death at sea rather than conform to those stifling conditions.

The colonies had hardly begun when the mother country began imposing heavy taxation. This started an intense chain reaction for freedom. A group of highly dedicated and trustworthy citizens began talking about a dream, the shape of what could and should be. With their faith as a foundation they designed the constitution and bound themselves together in a sacred covenant. They agreed that their experiment, which would be protected by fair play and due process under law, was of such importance that they would give their lives, fortunes, and sacred honor for it.

In the beginning the populace was so busy with work, family, survival, and the adventure of exploring the new world that they neglected their original dreams. Some thought dictators were essential. Some wanted no government at all. But as you know, the vivid dreams of the few prevailed. A convention was called. The colonies sent delegations to forge a system of agreements by which the impossible could be accomplished. Conflicts were intense. The rugged individuals did not want to compromise on anything. Issues would be debated for days. The pride of territory was already strong.

The design of the convention provided for freedom, full debate, and fair play for all. No decisions were forced upon others. Many times tempers flared, colonies threatened to pull out, and impossible demands were made, but the Madisons, Franklins, Adamses, Jeffersons, Hancocks, and all the rest hammered out the basic form by which an incredible experiment began.

As Abraham Lincoln was to say later, this is a "government of the people, by the people and for the people." But that nation of people went through some serious struggles before they learned to work together. External pressures and internal conflicts threatened their survival. No one knew whether the constitutional design was sturdy enough to handle the immaturity and demands of these unskilled people. No one knew whether human nature was pure enough to endure the strains of democracy. The Frenchman de Tocqueville called it a great experiment. Can a nation preserve the balance between freedom and responsibility? Some people thought it was preposterous to expect citizens to do what was necessary to keep a nation strong. They thought that to have unity, individual freedom must be eliminated.

Many times these founding fathers sought for the spiritual stamina to continue. They searched in the annals of human history for clues about human nature. They pondered the sacred worth of the individual and the desire of the group to survive in its environment. They sought for evidence of divine support. When their convictions were clear, they found the faith to attempt this bold new venture and committed themselves and their children to the greatest experiment of all times.

Religion gets involved when people attempt the impossible because it deals with the basic faith and convictions by which we live. People who take their beliefs seriously find a great kinship with another group of people who long ago attempted the unthinkable. The experience of the Hebrews in forming a nation in the desert wastelands of the Middle East staggers the mind. When this heroic group of people faced the insurmountable odds, they created a faith that has inspired people in every generation since. Their experience with the raw edges of life, as recorded in the Bible, has given us insight into how we too may face impossible odds.

I have been reading some of those early records of

courage found in the Bible. Archaeology records the environment out of which this faith was born. Covenants, already common during Abraham's day, were treaties that bound the inferior to the superior with elaborate clauses. These suzerainty treaties required little of the powerful king, but from his subjects he demanded total obedience, exorbitant taxes, and absolute support. Failure to obey brought death to the entire tribe. The condition of the world was so precarious that no one thought of trying to survive without a pact with a powerful king. Abraham, however, without a human treaty, left Haran for the uncharted unknown. He left the familiar patterns of support and ventured into the future with nothing but a spiritual dream—a spiritual pilgrimage. His claim was that God promised to bless him so that he could be a blessing to others (Genesis 12). He gave his life to that dream. He journeyed by faith alone.

There followed in the wake of this mighty father of faith a group of people who also had dreams of land and kingdom. They needed a place to demonstrate this style of living. It took special courage for leaders to attempt those incredible feats against the astronomical odds, but Moses, by the grace of God, led the children of Israel into the covenant community in the wilderness.

The spiritual pilgrimage of Abraham and Moses set the stage for the scripture in chapter one of Joshua. Moses was getting old, and the dreams of entering the promised land were not yet accomplished. The new generation was demanding action; they were getting restless in the wilderness. So Moses called a national convention, described in Deuteronomy 31, during which time he acknowledged his impending death and declared that Joshua would be their new leader. That is when Joshua became anxious.

Joshua, as a young man, had always had an optimistic spirit. As a spy for Moses long ago, he saw how people could do things others thought impossible. But their lack of faith locked them in the wilderness for a generation. Joshua saw it and told them so. Fear paralyzed most of them.

Now those pessimistic peers were dead, the old leadership was stepping aside, and a new day was at hand. Joshua had all the responsibility of leading, inspiring, and guiding the nation. He exercised caution, for he had seen how blind and cowardly people often were. The book of Joshua describes how this ancient leader faced the seemingly impossible odds.

It is fascinating to me to see how quickly and succinctly the Bible passes by the agonizing emotions and the frustrating processes of decision making. In just a few verses the author summarizes the criteria that Joshua decided to use to govern the people, the desire he had to continue the dream of Moses, and the confidence he learned from the patriarchs.

Joshua was frightened and rightfully so. Decisions he made affected many people. He needed to be a wise and courageous leader. How does one get courage? The scriptures give us a clue. Joshua spent a lot of time getting things clear in his mind: reviewing the qualifications of the people, their cause, dreams, discipline, and courage. He examined the obstacles to this dream and developed a strategy by which the hopes God had given them could be achieved. Out of his prayer and reflection he gained the same confidence that Moses had had in God. Listen to the words again: "Be strong and of good courage; be not frightened, neither be dismayed; for the Lord your God is with you wherever you go" (Joshua 1:9).

Those inspiring words did not appear mysteriously,

they came directly from the mouth of Moses just a few days before, as Moses left his parting instructions to the people. He told them that Joshua would take them into the promised land. It was in that commissioning service for Joshua that he used those inspiring words which have helped so many of us face great impossibilities: "Be strong and of good courage, do not fear or be in dread of them: for it is the Lord your God who goes with you; he will not fail you or forsake you" (Deuteronomy 31:6).

Because those words represented the faith by which Israel was created, they inspired Joshua. He used them to encourage his men to be brave in battle; they were repeated when David directed Solomon to build the temple; and they were used by Hezekiah when Sennacherib gathered to do battle against Judea. They were also the words of Daniel and are common in the inspiring worship material of the Psalms.

We too need faith as we face seemingly impossible odds. What can one person do against billions? What can we do in the face of the frightening proliferation of hostilities, the narrow dogmatic philosophies and powerful groups who control the world? We are not in a position to build a new nation from scratch. Right now we do not have any new land that we can settle. These limitations only add to the pessimism and strain of our day. While hostilities in days past might lead to the deaths of hundreds, today they can destroy the world. We need to recover Joshua's faith.

The origins of Israel and America have much in common. Both nations grew out of intolerable oppression. The cry of the human spirit against injustice and slavery was heard by God. Our pain often prods us to act. Whether it is injustice, corruption, irresponsibility, or the need to do something about our health, family, or financial situation, most of us do not act until we have to. Oppression united the Hebrews to leave slavery, and inhumane treatment inspired the early Americans to declare their independence.

Both of these two revolutions shared a great dream. It is one thing to complain and criticize, but it is a far more important matter to imagine a better solution. In both, the community elected to live by a standard of laws, instead of the whims of tyrants. They sought for the common laws of God and pledged themselves to live by those laws. The standards of agreement, freely chosen by participants, represented agreements of the community about what ought to be. They might not know exactly how things would turn out, but they agreed upon the guidelines by which they could make decisions. They dreamed of fair procedures, the importance of people, common goals, and a way in which each person could have some influence. They sought to assure everyone that the rights of all persons would be protected and cherished.

Both nations also had leaders and people committed to make the dream work. The children of Israel were so excited about the new opportunity that they created a word of exultation that has never been translated into any other language: "Hallelujah"—praise the Lord. Miracles happen when people have a concentrated determination. Our pioneers had the determination to identify problems and propose solutions. The settlers who came later tended to resist change, assumed that what they had was permanent, or that what they had could be continued without effort. Moses noted this tendency in his speeches to Israel. The nation's laws were only good when each new generation had the same determination to find and do the will of God. The

Shema contained the secret: "You shall love the Lord your God with all your heart, and with all your soul, and with all your might" (Deuteronomy 6:5-6). We can have the form of freedom without the spirit of it. Communities accomplish the impossible when everyone gives the very best of his or her determined effort.

The early Hebrews and early Americans accomplished the impossible because as a group of people they saw obstacles as opportunities. As a result the creative energies of people were released, which made possible the settling of the Bible lands. In America, a model Constitution, bill of rights, and system of government was established. In addition its citizens have always attempted the impossible: the erection of the Empire State building, the construction of the Panama canal, the building of the Golden Gate Bridge, and the space shot to the moon. For people of determination, obstacles are just rocks of opportunity that must be overturned. When one solution doesn't work, ask more questions, propose different solutions, get a bigger perspective, talk it over with someone else, debate the problem, and be persistent. That is the same spirit of faith that Joshua received from Moses: "Be strong, do not be dismayed; you are not alone." Christians have long known the power of faith and the promise of prayer: "What ever you ask in my name I will give it." The world is full of secrets just waiting to be unlocked by us and used for the glory of God.

When we finally become convinced that something is of sufficient value that we will give our life for it, then we are ready to attempt the impossible. The founding fathers and the heros of the Bible found that God was working for good in all things. God is here. We are not alone. When the impossible odds are recognized, God emerges through the fog of confusion to guide and direct our affairs. It is at such times we find incredible resources that we never knew existed. As we learn to live with impossible odds, we find there is an eternal Friend who is with us.

Finally, those who are determined to face the impossible odds with faith gain inspiration from others of faith. There is a mutual communication network between people of faith. They question every assumption, explore every glimmer of truth, and give their very finest energy to enlarge their vision. They keep talking with any other person who is humbly questing for truth and is committed to follow the truth wherever it leads. Joshua found his inspiration in Moses' words and leadership. The American founding fathers received inspiration from the scriptures and from democratic experiments of nations like Rome and Greece where law and justice had been strong.

If we remain faithful to God when we face impossible odds, truth and love are more important than winning. The means is as important as the end; people are more important than things; and eternal truth is something for which we will live and die. When we face the deep questions of life we recognize our limitations, face the impossible odds, live with compassion and faith, and incredible miracles happen.

Our world's pessimism and fear need the faith-building inspiration of those who have lived before us. Like Joshua of old, we need to listen to the voice of eternity until we hear God say: "Be strong and of good courage; I will not fail you or forsake you."

Perhaps the most contemporary way of being faithful to that spirit is found in the catchphrase, "Bloom where you are planted." Be a beautiful specimen of faith, courage, and love right where you live and work. Bear good fruit. God uses blooms to bear good seeds. And while you may count the seeds in a bloom, you can never count the blooms in one seed. That is a fact of eternity.

CHAPTER VIII

THE ART OF
COPING WITH PAIN

One evening I received a call from a member of my congregation asking that I go quickly to another member's home. The urgency of the voice told me that something tragic had happened, but he would not say what it was over the phone. I raced to the home and rang the doobell. When the door opened, I saw that everyone was in tears and friends were helplessly trying to be pillars of strength. The children were pacing the floor, going from one adult to another. The police seemed unemotional and gentle, trying to understand the tragedy while dealing with their task at hand.

As soon as I was spotted, one of the family members slapped her hands on her hips, stopped crying, and shouted at me, "What kind of God do you represent that let this happen?" I did not know what had happened, but I understood the anger and grief expressed. I asked to be told about the problem. Then it came tumbling out. The family was sitting down to supper when they heard a noise outside the house. One of them had gone out to check and discovered someone in the yard. He shouted for the person to leave and gave chase. It ended with murder. When I arrived, all were in shock and disbelief.

The cry of the universe is all the same. Why? Why? Why? we ask. Physical and emotional pain come to most of us. It may be the persistent pain of arthritis, a chronic heart condition, or cancer. It may be a nagging emotional pain, a vague haunting shadow in the soul, or the stark brutality of the untimely loss of a loved one. Sooner or later we all face it. The whole human race struggles with the questions: Why death? Why disease? Why suffering? Why pain?

Physical pain has received the attention of professionals. It is a sign that something is wrong. The sensing devices of the body communicate the distress to other parts of the body as a call for help. The totality of the organism is mobilized for solving the problem. In the beginning we may have little awareness of the internal fight taking place between germs and the white corpuscles, but if the fight gets out of hand, the body may ache, the temperature rise, and we get the message: go to bed, get plenty of rest, and drink lots of liquids.

Emotional pain is experienced as anguish. Loss of loved ones cuts us off from the warmth of love and support. Sharing joys and sorrows gives us a sense of self-worth and importance, and that is threatened by the death of a loved one. Sometimes we feel grief when one of our children gets married. We may convince ourselves that we gain a son or daughter, but at the same time our place of importance to the child may be diminished. The empty nest leaves us with emotional pain. Losing part of our body by surgery may create both physical and emotional pain.

There is also the pain of guilt. When our behavior—

what we did or did not do—brings pain to those we love, we experience guilt. It is often easier to suffer from others' wrongs or failures than from our own. Various experiments with monkeys have indicated that when one monkey is made responsible for the health and well-being of others the resulting stress produces ulcers and other physical problems. Persons who are in responsible positions and are sensitive to others' well-being often feel this kind of pain.

Another kind of pain arises when we fail. There is some deep drive within us to be in charge of ourselves. If we fall, we look around to see who saw us make a fool of ourselves. It pains us to say, "I couldn't do it." We know we were meant to do things, to work and make a contribution. However, when all our efforts end in failure, when everything we do has the opposite effect of our intentions, we experience pain.

Boredom is the pain that drives many to obsessions, compulsions, and hyperactivity. There are those who believe that the pain of meaninglessness, aloneness, emptiness is the driving force behind our obsessions with power, pleasure, and creativity. Our desire to escape from the pains of life explains much of our sickness.

Anthropologist Joseph Campbell reports that most cultures recognize a deep fracture in the human being's spirit that needs healing. The various expressions of worship found across the world indicate the longing of people for a reunion with the divine. The acts of sacrifice, the altars, the content of rituals, indicate the spiritual pain that exists. Until we find our peace with God there is a restlessness—a deep awareness that something is wrong. In one place the Bible calls that restlessness "the bottomless pit."

Augustine said that our hearts are restless until we find peace with the Lord.

Dr. Viktor Frankl said to a group of ministers in Dallas that the world tends to judge success on a horizontal plane from failure to success. "The deepest need is for a vertical relationship," he said. "The tragedy in life is that persons who succeed on the horizontal plane often end in despair, while the person with pain and failure often finds a sense of victory." That deep spiritual experience called despair is a serious pain. We want victory.

While growing up, some of us learned a stoic philosophy that taught us to ignore pain. It took me several years to get past the problem of overriding pain. If something had to be done, I would push the pain aside and with sheer willpower act as if it did not exist. Occasionally we may need to do that, but if it becomes a regular habit the sensing of pain is dulled so that we ignore real dangers to our health and life.

The measurement of pain is difficult, but some have a higher threshold of pain than others. It may be that some people relax more perfectly, or maybe their sensors work differently. For whatever reason, for some people pain is more debilitating than for others. For some, pain destroys their full potential, while for others it becomes the driving force that makes them productive. It often robs us of happiness and threatens our self-worth and productivity.

Pain is so universal that it has received the attention of thoughtful people through the ages. One of the great poems in the Bible was written about it. This dramatic poem argues against the pervasive explanation that suffering and pain are the results of sin. The commonly accepted wisdom argued: the righteous prosper, the sinful suffer. This biblical poem of Job, well known before the time of King David, was written about the year 600 B.C. to address the question: Why do good people suffer?

Job is a blameless and upright man. Furthermore, with sensitive devotion, he resists every kind of evil. By all the standards of prosperity he is the richest man in the east—which means that everyone also considers him the most righteous. He has the perfect number of sons and daughters (seven sons and three daughters). He has endless possessions (seven thousand sheep, three thousand camels, five hundred oxen, five hundred donkeys, and a great many servants). Job expresses his righteousness in his acts of worship, his kindness to others, and his devotion to his family. He worships God daily with burnt offerings, just in case someone might have sinned accidentally. Job is faithful.

The story then proceeds to describe how tragedy strikes. Job loses all his children, his servants, and his possessions. He loses everything. Even with this collapse, he is confident and does not sin. His only response is, "I came into the world naked and I leave the world naked; blessed be the name of the Lord, anyway."

Job is next reduced to "loathsome sores." He is struck with such incurable misery that he sits in ashes and uses a potsherd to scratch himself. At this point his wife gives up on God and tells Job that his religion is a waste of time. She advises him, "Curse God, and die." Job firmly refuses, telling her that life has some good and it has some bad. You have to accept the bitter with the sweet.

Job's plight reaches the ears of his distant friends who come at their own expense to counsel him through his pain and anguish. They are especially sympathetic and wail for his misery as if it were their own. They identify with him. They listen to Job cry out,

"Why was I ever born?" The friends ask if they can be candid with him; but before Job can answer, they insist that whether he likes it or not they must tell him the truth. (I always dread people like that.) Then they declare their miserable philosophy that everyone knows that "vexation kills the fool, and jealousy slays the simple." They advise Job to "seek God" and commit his cause to him. "Let God purge you of your sin. God does not reject blameless people," they continue (Job 8; my paraphrase).

Job recognizes the impossibility of finite creatures like us being blameless before God, but he denies deserving this suffering and pain. He prays that his friends will stop adding to his misery through their accusations. "Have mercy," Job pleads. "I'm in misery, can't you see?"

Relentlessly they insist that Job is mocking God because he stubbornly refuses to admit that his sin deserves this punishment. Job angrily replies: "I suppose you think that wisdom will die with you. I have understanding as well as you; I am not inferior to you. Leave me alone," he demands helplessly.

Finally, the only consolation Job finds is faith. He cannot see God, but he believes that if God could be found then reason and justice would prevail. Job only believes that somewhere in the great universe "my Redeemer lives . . . and . . . (someday) from my flesh I shall see God." His friends reject his faith, but Job persists, "I know that God is good and in the greatness of his power, he would give heed to me. I am willing to be judged by him" (Job 23:1-6, paraphrased).

Job enumerates his righteousness. He is pure of heart, he has not walked with falsehood, he is sexually pure, he has never been harsh to the servants, he has given to all the poor who asked for help, he has not trusted in gold, and he has never rejoiced at the ruin of his enemies (Job 31). While Job has few answers, he clearly contends he has done nothing to deserve these tragedies.

In the book of Job, as well as elsewhere, people have sought answers to the question of the theological understanding of pain.

The claim is made by some that this is a senseless world, cold and heartless. We must put up with the pain as best we can. Others tell us the pain is the result of our original sin. We are paying the penalty of our godlessness; pain is God's way of purifying us. Occasionally someone tells us that the pain is not real, it is just in our heads.

The very efforts to understand pain give us a clue about how intense pain can be. Philosophies of life get formed around the problem of pain and suffering.

The question of Job is a universal one: Why do good people suffer? Without answering the problem, the poem does make it clear that God is on the other side of our questions. Asking questions and facing the issues of life is essential. The questions may be haunting and frightening, but reality demands they be dealt with.

Dealing with pain presents theological problems, but first we need some practical skills by which we may successfully cope with it. From Job we can gain some clues about doing that.

Job acknowledges his feelings about pain. There were positive ones and negative ones. Job experienced anger and frustration and expressed it. Pain thrust on Job questions of life and death that he could no longer ignore. The whole event generated intense feelings. Feelings are not right or wrong, they are the sensors that

measure the human emotions like thermometers
measure the temperature of our environment.

Pain generally tells us something is wrong, even
though we may have a hard time knowing just what.
Listening to the signals that our bodies, minds, and
spirits send us, keeps us in touch with reality. Pain is
the body's way of telling us we need help. If we can't
find it by ourselves, then we need to find a
professional who can help us.

It was the proprietor of a cleaning establishment
who helped me see pain as God's gift. He was a
paraplegic. His mood and accommodating spirit made
him the joy of our neighborhood. As the months went
by, his wife told me about the alertness required to
maintain his health. He felt no pain. My first thoughts
were, I wish I were free from pain. Then she described
how she had to monitor his temperature and visually
check for signs that might indicate sickness—bruises,
cuts, sores, and such. He would feel nothing. He could
get seriously ill before anyone even knew about it.
Then I saw that pain is a very valuable gift—a sort of
early warning signal that saves our lives.

But there are pains we cannot relieve or avoid. When
that time comes nothing substitutes for a sympathetic
friend. Job had none. We find consolation and support
in people who understand us, who listen to us, and
who walk with us through our pains and humbly
pursue with us those questions which Ecclesiastes says
cannot finally be answered. The more like Christ they
are the better. Friendship is a channel by which God's
love is made accessible to us. Seek out and develop
friendship. It is God's design for help.

Job's approach to pain was good. He focused on his
resources. He had made some good observations
about life, he still had his mental capacity, and he had

his faith in God. His struggle with the question has made a significant contribution to our insights about suffering. He used the event to make a positive contribution to others, just as some contribute through music, the arts, and drama. Most do it by sensitive understanding. When the pain could not be removed, Job transformed it into something useful through his faith (Job 29).

My grandfather, who cherished being able to do everything around the farm, dreaded the future facing him when at eighty-two the doctor told him that he had cancer. A few days later, at our Thanksgiving dinner, Granddad was asked to give the Thanksgiving prayer. He bowed his head, and he began to give thanks for all that had been. I heard the tremor in his voice as he concluded the prayer, "And loving father, as we face the great unknown, help us to know we are not alone." It was hard to listen to his emotions then, but from his prayer I learned a valuable lesson about living and dying. The faith I saw in him has sustained me through almost twenty-five years of various kinds of pain and anguish. Our loving confidence in God stays with us, helps us, and gives us grace to help others as well.

None of us like pain, but it is part of life. Sometimes we can see what is wrong and fix it. There are times when we must be brave and bear our own burdens. There are times to bear one another's burdens and fulfill the law of Christ. There are times when we can do nothing but cast our anxieties on the Lord, because only God can sustain us.

We keep asking radical questions until we can see through the pain to the goodness and strength of God. Then we discover, as Job did, that we live and endure by the grace of God. We are never alone.

CHAPTER IX

DEALING WITH
RAGE AND SELF-PITY

I have known only one person in my lifetime who has denied ever having experienced rage and self-pity. By rage I mean that intense outward expression of anger. By self-pity I mean the internalized manifestation of anger. Most of us must deal with the emotion of anger as well as its symptoms. Generally this anger arises because some conflict has gotten out of hand and we feel threatened.

In a business magazine I read a headline "Anger, the Greatest Problem in Productivity." Anger is an emotion found in every person. It is expressed in numerous ways. Information is withheld, cooperation is denied, and needed communication is prevented because someone is angry with another. Reputations are ruined, careers broken, and friendships destroyed by it. Families who have been close for many years are destroyed by unhandled anger and uncontrolled rage.

What is a person to do? Anger does exist in all of us. If we feel that anger is wrong it may lead us to repress our feelings. When we do that we can find ourselves depressed, despondent, and tense, unaware of the reason. But to express rage without restraint brings death to others. The rise of violence in our society reminds us of the need to become aware of our emotions and manage our conflicts better.

As a minister with a diversity of training and experience, I am always surprised by my own emotions. I keep thinking that I have a rational understanding of my emotions and possess coping skills; therefore I should not have any of these emotions. Some people in my congregation act and speak as if they too think I should be emotionless. But let me share a part of reality from my own life.

Martha and I have been married almost thirty years. I counsel and believe that all of us should work at improving our marriages because life changes and it is so easy to take things for granted. Our own philosophy prompted us to use David and Vera Mace's book *How to Have a Happy Marriage* (Abingdon Festival book, 1979). The book outlines a six-week contract, with carefully outlined procedures for communicating, growing, and handling conflict. One exercise required ten minutes of thinking about some particular emotion and sharing our thoughts with each other. We chose to think about anger. We were to think about when we got angry, how we felt, and how we acted when we were angry. After ten minutes I was totally unable to think of anyone with whom I was angry. When Martha shared her feelings about anger, I noted that she felt worse than I because she had anger but I did not. Always having been a good Pharisee, I knew my tendency to hide things from myself; so I thought even longer. Suddenly to my consciousness came a scene that I disliked, so I tried to push it from my mind. The more I thought, the more I knew I must share it. The Mace exercises had given me some helpful advice about how to do this without doing harm to the other person, so I tried.

"Martha," I started, "I don't like what I've just discovered. I have some angry feelings about you. I don't like them. I'm not proud of them. Will you let me share them without feeling it is your problem?" She agreed, and I continued to tell her about my emotions, trying not to blame her for them. As soon as I shared my feelings with her, I discovered that I was harboring other hidden angers, self-pity, and my own frustrations. It took about ten minutes to get it out. When I finished and lay back on my pillow I found the first freedom from the tremendous tension I had felt for nearly two weeks. We both felt better, had new insights, and felt closer than ever. Who would have suspected that this inner anger was sapping my energy, making me a nervous wreck, and preventing my enjoyment of life? I found it hard to realize that sharing the emotions with a good listener was all I needed to be in charge of myself again. "Shouldn't something else be done?" I wondered.

The failure to feel good about ourselves produces its own amount of anger, which may surface either as rage or as self-pity. Someone described the problem this way, "If the world hates you, that is cruel; if it persecutes you, that is terrible; but if you can't stand yourself, that is unbearable." Sometimes we feel so ashamed about our anger that we repress it to the point that we don't know it is there. Anger, however, is normal and healthy. It is not meant to be used to dominate others against their will, nor should it be turned inward with denial. It must be handled and channeled. It is the only way to feel good about ourselves again.

Our limitations may be a source of considerable

anger. We do not like the thought of dying. We do not like the limitations our bodies or our communities place on us. We do not like to fail or sin. These inner conflicts stir up our emotions, and our emotions stir up conflicts. We must deal with our own mortality and limitations.

Some deny that they have anger. They do not ask for what they want and need. They do not assert themselves. When others seem to be insensitive and disregard them, their emotions become so strong internally that they may feel that they have no other choice but to check out of life. Berating them does no good; they already hate themselves. This anger turned inward as self-blame and self-pity is so vengeful it will not even let the person admit angry feelings toward others, but will be seen as self-pity. When we can admit only that we are hurt, we tend to deny that the emotion is really anger. When we do this we need help in facing our emotions and skill in handling them constructively.

If we continue to deny our feelings of anger, we tend to get sick, feel hopeless, and drop out. Like the turtle, we go underground and wait until things get warmer and safer. This withdrawal solves nothing and robs the world of some great minds and sensitive spirits.

Those who think anger and self-pity should not exist in religious people should recall with me the story of one of my favorite biblical heroes—Elijah. Israel's leaders saw the benefit of making a treaty with Phoenicia, which would give them both military and economic advantages. To accomplish this, marriage of the Phoenician king's daughter and the future king of Israel was arranged. Since the economic issues were considered primary and religion was considered insignificant to their enterprises, few thought the religious values of the Phoenicians would make any difference. In fact, their rituals, pageantry, and ethics seemed more earthy and practical than those of Israel.

Elijah, however, found this a serious blow to Israel's faith in the one invisible God. From the time of Moses they had made a covenant to be God's people and to practice the ways of justice, freedom, and order which the law gave them. Furthermore, the Lord demanded that attention be paid to the morals and ethics of relating to one another—the secret to a continuing society. Baal, on the other hand, prescribed certain ceremonies that promised fertility, rain, happiness, and so forth. For Elijah, baalism was paganism, superstition, and failure to face reality. It was regression of the worst kind, and he said so.

After several years of trying to persuade people, his indignation led to a well-designed strategy. Some counseled him to let both religions exist side by side, but Elijah declared they were incompatible. Face the truth and live with it, he declared. "Quit hopping from one foot to the other," he shouted. "If God is God, serve him; if Baal is God, serve him" (I Kings 18:21; paraphrase). A contest on Mount Carmel was arranged to see which was truly God.

The book of I Kings tells how the Lord sent fire to consume the sacrifice of Elijah, who thereby won the contest. Elijah said the Lord is God and all Baal priests should be eliminated. He gleefully conducted a massive slaughter. Queen Jezebel, the chief advocate of Baalism, went into a rage and swore she would kill Elijah in twenty-four hours.

That is the setting for this scene. Elijah had run for his life nonstop to Beer-Sheba, in Judah, and collapsed under a broom tree. When he awoke, he was so depressed he wanted to die. He took time to rest, was convinced to eat, and then spent forty days in the wilderness moping around as a refugee. Finally he returned to the source of Israel's beginnings, Mt. Sinai (Horeb), where he found a cave for protection.

Here, a voice said, "What are you doing here, Elijah?" By this time, Elijah was full of self-pity and replied pathetically: "I have been very jealous for the Lord. . . . The people of Israel have forsaken thy covenant, thrown down thy altars, . . . slain thy prophets. . . . I only am left; and they seek my life" (I Kings 19:10).

Can you feel Elijah's emotion? He was angry. The most sacred things in the world had been neglected. He was afraid of the future. When Elijah was asked what was wrong, he erupted with the anger he had been holding inside. That angel who was ministering to him really heard it all.

This angel presented no argument. Every effort was made to get all the anger out and deal with the heart of the matter. I think the Bible condenses the description of emotions into such brief sentences we miss them. Can you picture Elijah elaborating on all the evil that is going on in the society? Can you hear him express disgust with the nation's immorality and those who ignored their vows to God. Can't you hear him blast the weak leadership in the government and the economic barons who are getting rich, telling religion to tend to its own business?

Now, most of us are tempted to tell Elijah he got himself in this fix because he let his anger erupt into murderous rage. But his counselor did not remind him of the Baal priests he murdered, nor of his past sins and failures. The angel just asked questions and listened.

This messenger dealt not only with his anger, but also with his fear. In fact, fear is often an emotion that is underneath our anger. When we are afraid, adrenalin is pumped into our bloodstream and this chemical heightens our feeling of fear or anger. This accounts for the way we feel if we are afraid that our reputations, jobs, status, or futures will be lost. Elijah was fearful for his life, for the future of Israel, for the religious and moral convictions of the Hebrews, and he was afraid that if he didn't do something, everything would be lost. He thought he was doing what God wanted, but everything went wrong. The Lord's way was about to perish, the prophets were being killed, and no one was being faithful. That is what Elijah saw, that is what he thought, and that was how he felt.

When we encounter anger, we have to get past our fears of rejection, of being misunderstood, and past the personal feelings of guilt that affect our whole personality. Recognizing them, naming them, utilizing them for constructive purposes, are all ways of taking charge of them. If we don't take charge of them, they will take charge of us. As one recovering alcoholic said to me, "Those angers will eat you alive if you don't deal with them."

A careful look at the story demonstrates the way Elijah dealt with his rage and self-pity. It has some wisdom for us too. Elijah's messenger recognizes his basic need for rest and food. When everything comes at us at once, our emotional system gets overloaded. This is especially true if we have not taken care of the physical basics: getting proper exercise, rest, and food. A good balance of these basics would prevent many of our emotional problems, just as a healthy body prevents disease.

Fortunately God's messengers often appear just when we need them. They sometimes come in the form of a friend or relative, sometimes as a stranger, and sometimes as an enemy. God uses people to reveal his truth and love. In a very deep way we can all be priests to one another. These messengers do not solve our problems, they help us get back in touch with God.

There is healing in another thing Elijah did. He returned to the source of his basic faith. Sometimes we neglect the church, the heritage that is ours and those forebearers who gave so much for us. Elijah found it helpful to get back his basic beliefs and trust. At Mt. Horeb he remembered the stories of those early Hebrew leaders and pictured the conditions under which they lived. He dreamed again the dreams they had. He imagined the courage it took to overcome the obstacles they faced and the patience it took to manage all the conflicts of that complaining, blind, insensitive group of ex-slaves. He could no doubt recall the fickleness of people as one day they would shout "Hallelujah" with excitement and the next day they would be overcome with grumbling. It helped him remember he was not alone.

By getting away from the conflict for a little while and coping with stress constructively, Elijah gained a new and bigger perspective on life. Conflict had the potential for growth in it; and when Elijah could accept his own condition, accepting the reality that many things were beyond his control, he got through his anger and self-pity to see the goodness of God.

The entrance to the throne of God was stormy for Elijah. He had experienced the stormy winds of hate. He had watched the mountains of God shake convulsively. He knew the fire of anger that burned in him and Jezebel. He shuddered before the experience but saw nothing of God in all this. When he quietly faced the realities of life, however, Elijah could hear the still small voice of God whispering words of encouragement and hope. God's voice makes all the difference in the world.

If Elijah thought the encounter with God was an end in itself, he was mistaken. Again the messenger of God spoke: "Elijah, you need to find some constructive way to express yourself." Elijah might have done it in art or music or drama, but in this particular case he began working with the future. By now, Elijah was convinced that he was not alone—there were still seven thousand worshipers who had not compromised their faith. So he took his authority and power and used his anger as the fuel to find and anoint a new king.

The emotional experiences that arise from anger are not meant to be dissipated in rage or self-pity, they are meant to be used for constructive purposes. We can reproduce our faith and vision in our children and grandchildren, and we can make the world a better place by disciplined action. Taking charge of anger prevents the destructive acts of rage and self-pity, but it may require the help of others.

Anger is a powerful fuel for action. A good balance of food, rest, and exercise helps us keep it under control. Keeping in touch with God's messengers, our heritage, and our own purpose on earth helps us channel it wisely. These stormy times can be the very experiences that make us stop long enough to hear the still small voice of God. God never lets us retreat to the cave of experience for long before he sends us right back into the world to be a blessing to others: do something constructive to prevent future problems; handle injustice better; plan more wisely. Rage and self-pity are unproductive uses of anger, but by the grace of God the healthy use of anger can be the energy by which we create a better world.

CHAPTER X

DEALING WITH INTERNAL CONFLICT

I have ulcers. Just saying those words makes me uncomfortable. Everyone knows that a preacher should be a paragon of health. I feel like keeping that image of myself private. Sometimes I think that I am the only one who has ulcers. Men are expected to be strong, brave, and unemotional. A mature person is supposed to be one who can handle every emotion.

This pesky problem first arose in college. After the doctor examined me for that burning sensation in my stomach, he asked me if I were worried about something. "No," I said. "I'm a very happy, carefree person." "Do you feel guilty about something you've done?" "No," I said, and then thought to myself, "There is no one more moral than I am. What's he getting at?" I wondered. Then he said, "Leonard, you have ulcers, and they are generally produced by anxiety. I want you to find out why you're anxious, but until then here is a prescription and a diet."

Living with anxiety and inner conflicts produces many problems for us—some physical, some mental, some social. It took time for me to recognize the connection, but I began making some discoveries about myself. I found just how many times I had to choose between pleasing others or doing what I wanted. When faced with these problems I would get a headache, my stomach would get tight, my hands would perspire, and I would get quiet—paralyzed with indecision.

Then I made another discovery as I began dating a 5'2" blonde who weighed 98 pounds. There was more love in that girl than I had ever known. Within a month I had no more trouble with ulcers. The relationship continued to grow, and eventually we married. Six months later, the ulcers appeared again. We were moving, going to seminary, accepting another church, leaving familiar surroundings, and wondering how to pay our bills.

Those turbulent occasions arose frequently in the first years of adulthood. Gradually I discovered that these conflicts were especially strong when someone expected more of me than I could produce. I thought I was supposed to be able to do everything.

Somewhere I had learned that a Christian was supposed to live a clean life, work hard, do the right things, pray, and attend church, and everything would be peaceful, without conflict. I stuck with that philosophy and tried to make it work, separating myself from every form of evil. I developed an impressive style of life, just like a good Pharisee, but I wanted something more.

While attending seminary at Southern Methodist University, I served two churches near Altus, Oklahoma. The pressure of school, church, and the arrival of a new baby added to my responsibility. My poor stress management skills made it worse. Because I was "nice," few people criticized me; but I sensed that things were not going well. There were some things I wanted and didn't know how to ask for them. There were criticisms that I wanted to make, but was afraid of destroying my future. There were conflicts in the congregation for which I blamed myself. I sensed a crisis coming to a head—something had to be done. The ulcers returned.

About this time my professor of counseling said, "Ulcers are caused because we are so hungry for love that we begin to eat on ourselves." That hunger for love described me. Yet, if I believed that God loved me, why did I have ulcers? Maybe I did not believe? But as a Christian and as a preacher I had to believe. Those thoughts confused me for a while, and I did not like the feelings that came with them.

Yet there was an undeniable hunger in my soul for love. My experience with my wife demonstrated it, my obsession with pleasing people proved it, and my avoidance of conflict exposed it. Leslie Weatherhead said "eating" can describe how we take into our bodies what we need for survival, but it can also describe the way we assuage our emotional needs. When we say, "I digested that," or when we listen to a person talking about things that concern us and say "I really ate that up," we are describing our spiritual needs. I found myself saying, "Feed me, Lord, until I want no more." Where was that banquet of love?

As I thought about love, I remembered how much I wanted the love of my family. I had it then, I am sure, but my highly structured life blinded me to its presence. I could see only the requirements to be good in everything I did. If I failed I felt rejected. When I tried to describe myself, no one seemed to understand. If I confessed that I felt like a "sinner," my friends would say, "That's not true, you are the most moral young man I know." I could see that my ethics and standards impressed people, but that only compounded the problem. What if they discovered the truth about me? Hiding that truth from them created the worst of maladies, phoniness.

The presence of these internal, barely recognized conflicts made me conclude that no one really understood me. Who wants to confess the feeling that his parents don't understand him? Who wants to admit how desperate he is for love?

Easy platitudes, preaching to myself, and the cheap solutions I read did no good. I kept wondering why people kept avoiding the pain I felt. Why can't someone talk about it somewhere? Am I the only person feeling this way? Why do they put preachers on pedestals?

Then I found hope from the Bible. The church had convinced me that the Scriptures revealed eternal truth. I remembered a preacher saying, early in my childhood, "If you get confused by life put yourself in the role of one of the participants in the Gospels, such as Mary, Peter, or Andrew, and read the Bible from their perspective." My life crisis made me willing to read it that way. But what role would I play?

As I sought for a role, I made a startling discovery. I was almost a perfect description of a Pharisee—but who wants to play that role? I resisted that thought, preferring a hero role—Peter, James, John, or Paul. Every choice was getting to be a crisis. I had to be honest. Even though they could not compare with Jesus, the Pharisees were good people. They were the leaders of society and the pillars of righteousness. They never missed worship—neither did I. They were avid participants in religion; I, too, had held every major role in church life. They were zealous for their faith, as I was; for I evangelistically recruited people and asked them if they were saved. I preached the rule of the "moral majority" and was bitterly critical of every form of immorality. I knew the Pharisees were disciplined. They were scrupulous about tithing, and so was I. I also knew that they could not admit that they had evil thoughts, vile emotions, and impure desires—and neither could I.

The Pharisees had an absolute devotion to tradition, as I did. They knew what was right and were disciplined to do it in spite of all obstacles. They had totally and thoroughly separated themselves from the evils of the world as well as from sinful people. I associated with sinful people only to convert them. I considered myself better than others. I was just as self-righteous as they. Why did I have these ulcers? Because I was so good, and I tried so hard? It didn't make sense.

There was one reason I could face this pharisaism in myself. At age fourteen I had experienced the love of God in a very forgiving way. While the freshness of that experience lasted only a couple of weeks, I could never deny the marvelous peace and joy I found then. It was God's free gift, totally apart from my efforts.

However, when I reached twenty-five, my inner conflicts were multiplying. Life was crumbling. Something had to be done. I decided to read the book of Luke in this make-believe role. As I read, I winced every time Jesus talked about the Pharisees. I heard him say that he came for the lost, and I felt his tenderness even as he talked about the behavior of the Pharisees. I pictured him caring for the crippled, the lame, and the immoral. I felt his touch, patiently loving those whose souls were wounded by life. I saw him put the man called "legion" back in his right mind. I heard him saying to the Pharisees that there is more to life than outward observance. I wanted to believe, but I rebelled at his defense of the immoral; I was incensed by his seeming permissiveness, and I could not comprehend what he meant when he said that morality was not the point of religion. I thought he should criticize those unsuccessful and deviant people. I did not agree with Jesus that my condemnation of others did positive harm to them and to myself.

Yet I knew that when I judged others it made me fear that I might be judged by God in the same way. That scared me. What if all my secrets, all my thoughts and desires were fully known? How could I possibly stand that? I surely didn't want any mind reader following me around. I was beginning to discover a lot of sinful things about myself.

Finally I came to the twenty-third chapter of Luke. I was now living the events. The Pharisees were advocating the crucifixion of any man who claimed to forgive sin. I joined them, because being easy on sin would surely increase lawlessness; the society would perish, and religion would be lost. It was not surprising to me that the Pharisees helped engineer the death sentence and pushed the Romans into granting it. It was a familiar argument—cruel public execution would be a major deterrent to people like Jesus. Fear would make sinners conform to the laws.

As I read Luke's Gospel, I pictured myself standing in front of the cross, feeling all that internal conflict about my own failures, and I watched Jesus die. At first I thought he deserved it; yet I could not deny his genuineness. He died as he lived—humbly, genuinely, always loving—forever caring. He expressed it to his mother, and I heard it in his voice as he cried, "My

God, why have you forsaken me?" I understood that feeling. I felt forsaken too. God, did I feel forsaken! Then he did the unbelievable. Despite all his pain, he noticed all those who were guilty for his crucifixion below. Then I heard him pray those incredible words again: "Father, forgive them, for they know not what they do."

Tears of unbelief came to my eyes. He understands. He knows my experience. He accepts me as I am. I did not have to believe anything, do anything, attempt anything, or achieve anything. It was a free gift of mercy and forgiveness that made me want to give him nothing but my best. Nowhere had I found that among my Pharisee friends. Nowhere had I found that reality or motivation to live. Noncondemning love! What a miracle of peace!

After reading the Gospel of Luke, I lay quietly on the bed for a long time, thinking: "What does this mean for me now?" "Can I really be myself and let others be themselves? Can I really accept my sins and theirs, trusting that God's mercy is big enough to save the world? What about morals and discipline? Shall I give that up?" The internal conflicts were still great, and the questions continued. Would I move into the future by faith, or would I return to my rigid, narrow, critical style? Would I preach at people or share life with them? How should I accept all those people with different ideas and cultures and positions?

The inner turmoil was reducing, even though the questions were increasing. Somehow Luke reported the love of Jesus in a way that I could receive it. I could not fathom his love, which prompted him to pray for his enemies while suffering such pain himself. That was the kind of love I really needed, and it was given in a very convincing way. There was enough evidence in those words to inspire me to believe. If God couldn't be trusted, who could be? Jesus trusted God and understood how emotions make Pharisees, like me, do destructive things. Those words and that witness became new life for me.

When we face inner conflicts, the hardest battle is getting an anchor to keep us steady in the midst of life. Finding assurance of God's love and eternal dependability has done that for people of faith through the ages. The witness of others, the testimony of the scripture, and the evidence through the centuries of Christian history point to this stable anchor.

Yet knowledge of God's love is not enough. There comes a time when we must commit ourselves to trust that it is so. It is the only way faith can be tested. The time finally comes for us to intentionally decide what we really do believe and what we will do. The moment of truth arrives, and we must choose. If we avoid the choices we may be led into obsessions, tyrannies, and greater fears. We never know the future for sure, but by faith we can see and shape the future, for it is the eye of the soul. We can face all things securely with faith and love.

For me, the forgiving, accepting love of God, which endured the cross, became incredible. It became the most objective reality I knew. It was too good to be true and too real not to be true. The evidence was convincing. I did not know where it would lead, but by faith I knew I could receive it. It was a banquet of love that fed the deepest needs of my spirit.

An experience with God's love does not solve all our problems. But it gives us stability and prompts us to search for harmony in all things. We constantly grow, test, and evaluate. As life changes, we change. We must constantly work to keep our ears tuned to recognize discord and resolve it into the harmony that God intended.

The offer of forgiveness, mercy, and acceptance found at the cross was more than a historic event for me; it became an experiential event. The result was a gradual changing of life so that I could face and accept my life's internal conflicts with a growing sense of self-acceptance. Also, it meant being better able to deal with others' acceptance or rejection of me.

As life moves from crisis to crisis, new understanding, insight, strength, and growth are required. Worries can be intentionally set aside. Fears can be examined. Morals can become a way of loving instead of a cause for condemnation. Acceptance, with truth, becomes a way of transforming life instead of irresponsible permissiveness. The experience of God's forgiveness and grace is the divine companionship that gives us courage to be real and openly face the sordidness of life without losing control.

Life has its new crises, but if you are surrounded by God's love, they become challenges to grow in faith and accept the larger responsibilities that come with age.

Seldom have the ulcers arisen again; but when they do, I know it is because I have allowed my responsibilities to increase faster than my awareness of God's love. Those are the times to retreat, acknowledge my emotions, and commit myself by faith into God's grace again.

God's grace is adequate for every occasion. By faith we have access to it, as described by John Newton's hymn "Amazing Grace."

Through many dangers, toils, and snares,
  I have already come;
'Tis grace hath brought me safe thus far,
  And grace will lead me home.

It is that grace which calms our fears, convinces us of God's dependable love, and leads us through the unpredictable future to our eternal destiny.

CHAPTER XI

LIVING
WITH UNCERTAINTIES

In the Broadway musical and the movie *Fiddler on the Roof,* Tevye sings about tradition. Everyone's role in life was established by tradition. We see him discover that the world is changing and that tradition no longer controls decision making. Tevye faces the ponderous question, How can one be certain which decision is right? "On the one hand this is true, but on the other hand the opposite seems to be true." That is the mood of our day.

At the present time, we are experiencing a resurgence of conservatism, that desire to conserve the values of the past. Back in the 1960s there was a rebellion against tradition which demanded change. *The Late Great Planet Earth* became one of the best-selling books in America. Hal Lindsey and others picture the end of the world and the cataclysmic battle of Armageddon in the valley of Megiddo. While his argument was dismissed by many people, it raised the question for the whole world, Are we going to survive all the problems that threaten to destroy us?

The great question behind all this is, What does God want to happen? Does God eagerly anticipate destroying all the sinners on the earth? Is there nothing we can do? Will God work to save the world again?

Even if we dismiss the fear of the end of the world as the typical end-of-the-century or end-of-the-millennium jitters, we still cannot avoid the questions about the purpose of life and how we are to make choices.

The world will not let us avoid our limitations and mortality. More and more people are becoming convinced that the world is in trouble. Unmanaged conflicts can destroy us; the unrestrained greed of the profit motive can consume us; permissiveness without responsibility will kill us; dogmatism with military arrogance can make slaves out of us; communism's insidious revolutionary nature can precipitate an eruption anywhere in the world; and the terrorists demonstrate their ability to intimidate even the most powerful nations.

How do we face all the uncertainties and the fear that these issues raise? Does God want us to give up and let ourselves decay?

The greatest question is, How should we face the great unknown? How do we make decisions when we have so few guidelines? How do we handle the enormous crisis?

Most of us remember the confidence we felt as children, when we had clear and certain answers. When we became adults the issues became much more difficult.

Earlier in this century, it was often the case that when a person learned a job, he would be secure in it the rest of his life. Some people had financial holdings that let them relax. It seems that in those days children had two parents, and the home was solid and secure. The community was stable and people knew and helped one another. Today frequent moving contributes to instability. Once, as far as Americans were concerned, democracy knew no rival; but the world is challenging every idea of human conviction. There was a time when Christians knew little about other religions, but today we are challenged regularly. We now face many conflicts, and they are often intense. We need some dependable guidelines for making decisions.

Many of the old patterns are not acceptable now. Once the father gave the orders, the husband told the wife, and the boss told the employee. Not so today. When the spaces were open and we were an agrarian society we could move as we pleased; and our own actions, thoughts, and behaviors had few consequences. But in an urban society we must strictly follow the orderly rules of the road to survive. There was a time when retirement was no problem—we didn't live that long. Today there are more people alive over sixty-five than ever reached that age in the history of the world. There was a time when the amount of energy we consumed did not matter. Today its scarcity and cost make it a real issue. Now the world must decide what to do with nuclear waste, terrorists, pollution, and the like. Furthermore, we must decide who will make the decisions and with what criteria.

We no longer enjoy the security of a smaller, slower world. Horse-and-buggy rules do not work on a freeway. We need better skills for making wise decisions.

A critical event in the life of the early church may shed some light on our problems. Go back with me and examine how the early church faced one big decision. As you remember, the disciples had spent three intense years with Jesus, who had been crucified, raised from the dead, and had ascended. The story of God's act brought enormous response at Pentecost, and the enthusiastic Christians began their program to tell the whole world. The book of Acts tells how Peter had gone on his first expedition to Joppa and met some people seriously ill whom he healed. This miraculous word spread; so Peter spent additional time on the seacoast in the home of Lydia. While he was there he faced a radical new choice that would affect the whole world.

Not far down the coast was a Roman seaport, Caesarea, named for Caesar Augustus by Herod. Under the procurators it became the capital of Palestine. Riots there between Jews and gentiles in A.D. 66 marked the beginning of the Jewish war against Rome. Its picturesque harbor, the impressive colonnade, and the concentration of power made it an important and crucial headquarters for the Romans and the center hated by the Jews.

Cornelius was a prominent centurian stationed at Caesarea, a gentile who was a very devout worshiper of God. When he approached Peter to talk about the new Christian faith, Peter had to decide whether gentiles could officially be part of the Christian church. As you know, Peter had grown up maintaining a strong separation between Jews and gentiles. The conflict was intensified because Peter had associated with Jesus, who proclaimed that everyone was included in God's love and that God rules the whole world, not just the Jewish people. Quickly Peter realized that if he accepted Cornelius it would be a great departure from the tradition he had known. As you read the passage in Acts, Luke says Peter was "inwardly perplexed." He had reason to be.

Notice the emotion in this experience. Peter was perplexed—uncertain. He wanted to be loyal to his Jewish heritage and reject the unclean gentiles, but he wanted to be loyal to Jesus and include them. Also he felt the responsibility of being the leader of the disciples. What guidelines should Peter have used to decide? No decision would be popular with everyone.

Peter may have been inspired by the words and actions of Jesus, which made faith in God a universal reality, but he had no experience exercising this faith, and his emotions pushed him strongly to stay with the old tradition. He wanted to face the new challenges, but the choices were difficult.

Peter's problem was which tradition to follow. The crucifixion demonstrated how wrong tradition can be. Furthermore, as a Christian leader, Peter recognized that all the followers of Jesus were full of Hebrew tradition. His decision, which had to be made without consultation, would affect them too. Did they have the capacity to change and accept gentiles as equals in the fellowship?

Through a vision from God, Peter made a bold decision. He welcomed Cornelius completely. To Peter's surprise, Cornelius found the joy of knowing God's mercy, as did many others. The barriers were removed, and all found the unity and joy of God's universal love. No one could have anticipted the unity that would come from this daring act of acceptance.

Peter's vision of what God wanted still came from the Scriptures. Being holy and pure was important. He could not ignore the demand of Ezra and Nehemiah for absolute separation from the gentiles. When Peter examined the tradition, he no doubt recognized that laws were given for a specific time and place. He also considered in his own mind the impact of his three years with Jesus. Now, at this moment, he was struggling for certainty.

With all Peter's uncertainty, he decided to live toward the wave of the future. His reasoning, based on all he knew, said Jesus was right. The people he led had to have a bigger view of life. The reign of God's kingdom was over the whole world. This kingdom included every race, every class, every country on the face of the earth. The time had come; a decision must be made, and he would be the first follower of Jesus ever to extend full and complete fellowship to a gentile. He acted, using the strength of his popularity in Joppa to declare a new era in the history of Judeo-Christian religion. There is one God, and citizenship in his kingdom would be universal.

Peter was surprised with the result and said in amazement: "I perceive that God shows no partiality." It always startles us to discover that God is impartial. We want him to favor us, whether we are Methodists, Catholics, Republicans, Socialists, or whatever. Peter says God accepts all who truly respect him and do what is right (Acts 10:35).

God does not want us to make decisions based on fear. "Perfect love casts out fear." Peter could have feared those who opposed him. That would have been understandable, but Peter's convictions had grown stronger: God made the world, and God is unwilling that any perish. The gospel is for everyone. "Whosoever will, may come." Peter had to manage the affairs of the Lord. He could not run just because the decision was tough; the tough decisions call for the greatest faithfulness.

Peter also concluded that "none are common." All people are eligible for the Kingdom. The universe is one. We cannot deny it. Emotionally, mentally, spiritually, physically, the differences between people are insignificant. The dream was begun, the theory was tested, and Christians began to put their faith into practice.

In our changing world we too want to be loyal to our traditions, to our values, to the familiar; yet we know that some changes must be made and we are not certain what to do. The approach of Peter in resolving his conflict speaks to us about finding the will of God and may help us find the way forward with certainty. Peter dealt with one issue at a time. There were many other matters pending, but he took the one of greatest priority—the one that was constantly in his mind and vision. Our world wants to solve all problems at once. We live in a day of instant cures. We want medicines that do it now. The problems before Peter were numerous, but he focused on this one clear issue with which he had been struggling for almost three years.

When I was an assistant minister, I asked the senior minister of a large city church, "How do you manage all these problems?" In his very human way, he said, "Sometimes I say to the Lord during my morning devotions, 'Lord, here, take them all back now and hand them to me one at a time.'" I asked another person, "How do you ever write a book?" His response was the same: "You write it one word at a time."

For several years I have searched the Scriptures, trying to understand the will of God. For a long time I imagined that finding God's will was something that happened. I was trying to understand why certain things happened. It should have been clear that God's will has to do with relationships. God wants our love, and wants us to love one another. That is what Peter discovered. Relationships are more important than traditions or fears, but that does not eliminate uncertainty.

I went to my own church tradition to see how we had historically made these decisions about what God wanted done. In the United Methodist *Book of Discipline* this is what I found.

1. We do not claim infallibility. God's spirit leads the church. God is active and present today—leading, guiding, and strengthening us. The *Discipline* says that no set of words, codes, creeds, confessions, or dogma is infallible. God's eternal word never has been or ever can be exhaustively expressed in any set of human words. It would be inconceivable that God could be described with twenty-six letters and forty-three sounds that we have in English. Furthermore, the fullness of God's will is not infallibly known by any living person or group of persons. It is unthinkable to teach that the wholeness of God's will could be reduced to the size of mortal men.

While dogmatism is rejected, we assert our confidence that God is infallibly leading the church today—strengthening, perfecting, and guiding it. We do not live by knowledge; we live by faith in the Holy Spirit. God created the church and can be trusted. No ecclesiastical authority enforces obedience to precisely stated propositions of truth. That would be tyranny.

2. To discern the will of God, there are four great lights we can use to guide us in making decisions. The core of our faith stands revealed in Scripture, is illumined by tradition, made vivid by personal experience, and can be confirmed by reason. It enlightened me to realize this principle for decision making is found in the book of Acts and was used by the early Christians.

3. Our third guide through uncertainty is the use of "conference," which is the collective wisdom of living Christian pastors, teachers, and people. Jointly we seek for the leadership of God's spirit and, despite the many tensions, jerks, and stops, God's will is made known. Methodists assert that, by conferring with one another, the Holy Spirit is working in us today—creating harmony, establishing the vital balance, and keeping the world stable.

Since God is at work in the world, we get clear guidance about what is expected on the earth by looking at the life of Jesus Christ. Jesus had two rules for living: Love God purely; love your neighbor as yourself. This was the guide Peter also used in making his decision. God is God of all creation and loves all people. We are to do the same. No longer are we searching for the will of God; our problem is fulfilling it.

Resolution of conflict requires that people of good will and common sense provide a system by which fair play is extended to all persons. We may not be certain about the details of behavior, but we are certain that God intends us to love all people in the world. In the bond of love, we are called upon to provide a way for the hopes, dreams, and differences of people to be discussed and resolved in an atmosphere of trust.

Facing uncertainties requires loyalty to the very best we know about life. We need to follow procedures for decision making that are tested and reliable. Also we need to have sufficient faith to accept the challenges of the new day.

As a prologue to the penetrating message of Henry Van Dyke's book *The Story of the Other Wise Man,* the following poem expresses our confidence in compassion and love. Van Dyke says:

Who seeks for heaven alone to save his soul,
May keep the path, but will not reach the goal;
While he who walks in love may wander far,
Yet God will bring him where the blessed are.

Human existence upon this earth has always been
very uncertain. We live by the "provide-ence" of God.
God's grace and Holy Spirit can be trusted to guide us
into all truth, just as it did Peter. Finally and ultimately,
we are dependent upon God's goodness, and we offer
ourselves in absolute loyalty to this hope.

CHAPTER XII

SUCCEEDING IN MANAGING CONFLICT

No sermon is ever finished; it is just delivered. No book is completed; it just ends. No life comes to a complete conclusion; we simply die and go on. Somehow there is eternity in our breast, and living in the midst of time, we can never get it all done, say it all, understand it all. In truth, we live in an unfinished world.

For humankind life rushes on to that immortal shore. The words of Ecclesiastes only remind us of what we know so very well. There is a time to be born, and there is a time to die. Oh, time, why do you not stand still? Why must you bring us change? Why must the clocks keep on running? Why cannot we get ourselves perfected? The seasons come and go, "sunrise, sunset"—and we move through the mystery of life. When we reach the finality of death, how will we know if we were successful?

We are all tempted by despair. We get sick and tired of being sick and tired. Time wears at us, and the body fails, the emotions grow weary; increased responsibility and broadened understanding of life's problems tempt us to cynicism and hopelessness. We try, but fail. We love, but get hate in return. We grant freedom, but it is used to undermine the whole society. We need to remember that we live in an imperfect world, a world where the struggle for order is in combat with the eruption of chaos.

Just the facing of this reality evokes a melancholy spirit, a sort of grief for our idealistic, utopian dreams. We do not want to be told that paradise does not exist in some place or some system or some group. We search for our Holy Grails, we continue to dream our impossible dreams, and we desperately want the paradise restored. Emotionally, we are haunted by this dream. We are like the man who got up in the night, went to the refrigerator, looked through the shelves knowing he wanted something but could not find it, so he closed the door and sadly went back to bed.

Sooner or later, we all must come to terms with the bitter realities of life. This is not a perfect world. It has its joys and its sorrows, its roses, its thorns. This conflict of the soul over what is and what ought to be torments us all very deeply. If we do not deal with it, it saps our life and keeps us from love or peace.

The preacher of Ecclesiastes doubts our ability to find out what God has done from the beginning. "I have seen the business that God has given to the sons of men to be busy with. He has made everything beautiful in its time; also he has put eternity into man's mind, yet so that he cannot find out what God has done from the beginning to the end" (Ecclesiastes 3:10-11). Can we find solutions to conflict? Will our questions ever be answered? Were the good old days eons ago? Are they now? Are they in the distant future? Or is this hope a cruel hoax?

Paul noticed the same common human mystery when he said, "I do not do the good I want, but the evil I do not want is what I do. . . . Wretched man that I am! Who will deliver me?" (Romans 7:19, 24). Here is the most brilliant mind of the early Christian church and the one whom most call the founder of the church, saying that he finds a raging conflict within his soul between what he is and what he wishes. If that is the best condition of life, then what does it mean to be successful?

I think that Paul recognizes that all of us live somewhere between our realities and our dreams, between this earth and the eternal, between what is and what might be, between the finite and the infinite, time and eternity, the mortal and the immortal.

In the first chapter of Genesis, we read, "The earth was without form and void, and darkness was upon the face of the deep" (Genesis 1:2). God's creative act was to bring order out of chaos. Genesis suggests that humanity has an important part in God's plan for the earth's management, because it is in process. God is active, bringing order out of chaos, and we are to be part of that effort.

When Paul writes about feeling "wretched," it must be put in contrast with his usual comments. While he considers himself the chief of sinners and knows the gross realities of life, he talks little about that. He is far too overwhelmed with God's goodness, mercy, and love in Jesus Christ. The peace he found in God was eternal and unshakable. "Giving thanks" is Paul's chief emphasis. Success in living is possible. The conflicts are not worthy to be compared to the glory found in Jesus Christ. What is it that Paul knows?

To the Romans, he declares that we can rejoice in our sufferings because they help us grow. He is convinced that, no matter how dark the deeds done to us, God is present working for good. To verify his right to advocate this faith, he describes how he has been beaten, shipwrecked, left for dead, and has endured every imaginable kind of danger. God's grace is sufficient for every problem, he boasts. His most common phrase is to "give thanks always." Rejoice in the Lord. Be of good cheer.

J. Guild Wood made me an "adopted student" when I was in college. One day I was seeking Dr. Wood's guidance through a personal struggle. Instead of answering directly, he told a story about his early childhood as a son of a missionary in India. There, he would watch the beautiful butterflies wriggling to get out of their cocoons. Compassionately, he sought to reduce their struggles. Using the doctor's scapel, he cut the cocoon very gently. "To our amazement, every butterfly we helped was crippled for life," Dr. Wood declared. "Leonard," he said, "struggle and conflict are good. It takes that to keep us healthy." "Give thanks in all things," Paul advises.

Another way Paul dealt with his wretchedness was to recognize our growth. "We are not what we were and we are not what we shall be." Paul more clearly describes his basic belief about how to live in his letter to the Philippians. "Not that I have already obtained this or am already perfect; but I press on to make it my own, because Christ Jesus has made me his own. . . . I press on toward the goal. . . . Let those of us who are mature be thus minded and if in anything you are otherwise minded, God will reveal that also to you" (Philippians 3:12, 14, 15). We do not claim perfection;

we are faithful with what we do have, growing to the maturity seen in Jesus Christ.

Paul takes this wretchedness seriously, recalling how he consented to the stoning of Stephen. Yet the forgiveness from God that he found through the death of Christ on the cross grips him. It is God's love for him in his wretchedness that prompts him to present his body "as a living sacrifice, holy and acceptable to God, which is your spiritual worship" (Romans 12:1). He calls for us to do the same.

Paul genuinely credits God for all his achievements. It is always God's grace, received through faith, that works miracles. God works in and through all the conflicts of life to make all things work for good. Paul works so tirelessly because of the way Jesus emptied himself totally in love. What Paul saw in the cross was love poured out for us without reserve, even though we are wretched and sinful. Jesus endured every insult to win us back to God. It is that love that lets Paul acknowledge his failure and wretchedness, without wallowing in self-pity and self-recrimination.

In another letter, Paul talks about the best way to handle division among people and other conflicts. Love never ends. Paul said we are successful in facing and handling conflict when we do not give up. We may not live it perfectly yet, but the future belongs to those who do not give up. That is what Paul means by patience. What we give is not our own, it is Christ loving through us. We are to be instruments of God's grace.

In the midst of conflicts, it helps me to believe that nothing good is ever wasted. That is the way Paul faced the whole of life. Love is never wasted. Truth is never wasted. We will reap if we do not faint. God is victorious. The Lord has had and will have the last word. We are to be faithful! What we offer the Lord is never lost.

When our daughter was a student at Oklahoma City University, she became engaged and was given a beautiful ring by her fiance to symbolize their love. A few months later, Mary Len laid the ring down, and it was stolen. Though she shed many tears, offered a generous reward, and was joined by many friends in searching for the ring, it could not be found. She was embarrassed, humiliated, angered, and grieved. During her grief her grandmother said, "Nothing is ever lost in the Lord, Mary Len." She took that seriously in her prayers. One day, more than seven months later, one of her friends came running to her room shouting, "Mary Len, Mary Len, is this your ring?" With dancing and shouts of joy they celebrated its discovery and rehearsed again and again how her friend had found the ring downstairs in one of the community restrooms.

A few days later Mary Len saw a note on the dorm bulletin board announcing that a fellow student, Mamie, had lost a diamond ring. Fearing that both had a claim to the same ring, Mary Len stopped by Mamie's room, where she heard the rest of the story.

Mamie's mother had found the ring on another college campus in the city, and although she had advertised trying to locate the owner, no one had claimed it. She gave it to Mamie as part of her high school graduation gift.

Mamie confessed to Mary Len that she had never felt right about wearing a ring that obviously belonged to someone else. She was pleased that after the ring had been lost by three different people it was now back into the hands of the original owner.

Was all this simple coincidence? Mary Len is convinced that it was more, saying, "Nothing is ever lost in the Lord." Paul joins her in that celebration too: "If God is for us, who can be against us?" We are never lost to the Lord. God can be trusted in life and for eternity.

Love given is never wasted either. For some people the cross was a waste, but for Paul it was the power of God for salvation. It was the sign of successful management of conflict. Jesus had kept the faith, he was faithful to the end, and God raised him up as evidence that love is never wasted.

We love because we have been loved so perfectly, Paul says. The only major conflict has already been resolved, for in Christ we have been reconciled to God. The peace is won. All we do is receive the abundance of that grace and put that love into practice.

The faith I proclaim is a gospel of hope. It declares a God who provides the tensions in life by which we may grow, by which we mature, by which we become co-workers with eternity. It is a confidence that death is not the end. Through the power of the Resurrection we are given a lively hope now and eternally. No failure is final, no defeat is ultimate, and even the sins of the world are put in remission by the power of God's love. We are not yet perfect, but we press on to the goal of perfect love.

From Paul's discussion about the faith, let me summarize what it means to be successful in managing conflict.

1. We are successful not because of our achievements but because we are faithfully involved. We are called to conflict. We do not run from conflicts; but if we are faithful, we give our lives that the love of God may reign supreme. As we deal with others, we deal openly and fairly with all concerned. When we are loving in relationships, as Christ was, we are properly involved.

2. We are successful when we live with integrity. We seek to let nothing but love and good will control our lives, despite the emergence of emotions to the contrary. While in reality we cannot attain perfection, when we fail we ask for forgiveness. When we hurt others we make restitution if we can. Despite the clumsiness of life, the only successful conflict resolution is found when we keep our integrity—we do the best we can in love.

3. The third test of success is peace—shalom. That is not just the absence of war, it is peace in the realm. While there may be misunderstandings and tensions in every group, we work consistently to maintain an atmosphere where everyone is important. We struggle to design ways of living together where mutual faith and respect are current. When we act in purity of love, we are not defensive and we feel free. The Gospel writers distinguished this way of life from the bitterness of obsessive ambition and achievement. If we are successful in conflict, we can agree with Jesus that "my yoke is easy, and my burden is light." Peace is a result of integrity.

4. Conflict is managed when there is movement toward more consistent harmony and balance. There is no harmony without tension. Success is not the absence of conflict, it is the harmony we produce from the tensions. Harmony is the difference between organized sound and noise. Balance is the difference between walking and falling. The life of grace is not the absence of conflict, but balance. The word "grace" suggests doing the gracious thing in the most awkward of circumstances.

5. Conflict is being managed when there is a movement toward unity in diversity. Unity is the sense of order in the whole nature of things. It is this order toward which Paul sees God working. Where God reigns there is oneness, order, and harmony. There is no distinction and no partiality between people. We are all part of one another and are to live that way.

6. When the final conflict comes and we depart this earth, we are successful if we can face death peacefully, knowing that we have not lived in vain and that death is not the end. Faith is the eye by which we see the eternal now. One woman, talking about dying of cancer, said: "Dying is not that much different from living. Life consists of making choices. We give up childhood to become adults. We die to our relationship with our parents in order to become married; we die to our selfish interest to have children; and we die to a lesser good to live to a greater good." It is by the handling of all the conflicts of life's little deaths that the ultimate one is also seen to be in the gracious hand of God. Whether we live or whether we die, we are the Lord's.

When John Wesley came to the end of his eventful life, he read the Scriptures about the grace of God and then rose in bed to say in a loud, clear voice so that all could hear: "The best of all is, God is with us."

At every funeral service I join the family in tears and grief, but as I stand there I keep repeating our eternal hope when I say the grave is not all there is. There is more of God's grace to come. We have only begun to understand God's truth. We have barely scratched the surface of God's wisdom and hardly know anything of

God's love. Eyes have not seen, ears have not heard, and hearts have not perceived what shall be. The writer of John was right when he said he heard the Lord saying, "Come up higher." There is so much more to come.

In the conflicts of life, external, internal, and eternal, we are more than conquerors through God who loves us. Thanks be to God.

EPILOGUE

It is not enough to say "Peace, peace." We need to gain skills, insights, and disciplines to work together in the world. This epilogue is a theological reflection upon my personal pilgrimage. These final words represent the stages in my learning, propose ways by which we may relate to others when we are in conflict, and utilize the wisdom of theological insights.

In order to test and maximize my insights from my pilgrimage through conflict I have used some important theological tools that have helped me see through the conflict to the goodness of God. Why should any conflict be wasted? To ensure the reliability of my learnings I have sought to test my conclusions by God's Truth revealed in Scripture, illuminated by tradition, made vivid in experience, and tested by reason. These conclusions are the founding insights upon which the sermons are based.

The first ten years of my life were built upon the "winner take all" philosophy. In the little two-room school I whipped every boy to become "king of the mountain." I loved the superiority and control. When I was ten a new seventh-grade boy enrolled in school and soon whipped me, using a hammerlock on my neck that pained me for many days. That pain forced me to ask a life-changing question: Had I hurt others as much as he hurt me?

Another learning took place in the fifth grade when a neighbor boy stole my property and sold it. In return I wrestled him to the ground and poured dirt in his face. The next day he told me that his mother said I was going to hell for what I had done. That frightened me. I ran to my theological consultants, my parents, and asked them if he was right. They assured me of God's grace, but for weeks I dreamed of houses on fire and feared retribution. I concluded that God did not like fights.

For several years following, I sought to avoid conflict, but sometimes it seemed unavoidable. As an adolescent I felt the tensions between insisting on my own way and pleasing others. Guilt about my feelings was intense. I hated conflict as well as those who created it, but I could not say anything.

My emotional struggle climaxed when I attended a communion service where the liturgist was a minister I disliked intensely. I felt justified in my dislike, and guilty about my feelings, especially when I heard the ritual's demand for reconciliation. How can we adults deal with conflicts? What does God expect? I decided that the secret was in loving others and I would grow by doing three things: (1) by regularly reviewing my actions before God, (2) by deciding what values we ought to preserve, and (3) by terminating bad behavior in my life. The task was much more difficult than I had realized.

Seminary helped me accumulate a vast knowledge

of the conflict in the Bible and tradition. It gave me opportunity to reflect on the meaning of my own conflict theologically, and helped me understand the role of the minister: (1) to teach and preach the Word, (2) administer the sacraments, and (3) be responsible for order in the church. I failed to understand that creating order in the church means to manage conflict. My seminary emphasized the importance of being a prophet—telling people the truth about what God was doing and going to do in this world of sin. How could I know that for sure? If I was critical, it generated more conflict.

As I now reflect upon these early experiences I realize how confused I was. I had contradictory expectations. The tension was made bearable by the church's message that God's grace accepted us as we are, but I yearned for more insight.

Following seminary I assumed major responsibilities in youth work at the Mt. Sequoyah Assembly, in Fayetteville, Arkansas. We brought youth leaders from eight states to our training event, "The Church in Dialogue." Our purpose was to help the youth experience Christian community, learn the Scriptures, discover the Holy Spirit's leading, and make commitments to correct the world's injustices. We created the organization, developed some group skills, secured program materials, and divided the youth into fifteen groups of twenty persons. Unintentionally we created intense conflicts in these groups.

The get-acquainted period went well. There was a common bond: they were talented, Christian, dedicated leaders. They shared their abilities, joys, cultures, convictions, and dreams. Happiness was like Paradise—the garden of Eden. Love was abundant.

About the third day, major conflicts erupted. Strong

persons battled for recognition. Disagreements were heated, emotions rose, feelings became raw. Leaders were blamed, and some youth wanted to go home. The conflict threatened the continuation of the workshops.

Fortunately we scheduled a time to deal with feelings and relationships. As leaders we sought to present insights from the Bible to help them learn what God had done and was doing to create community. Finally, the participants began to hear the chance of learning, forgiveness, and understanding. The resultant reconciliation welded them together with such affection they wanted to stay on the mountaintop forever. Groups that did not learn the skills and theological insights of dealing with conflict disintegrated.

Two learnings emerged from these events: that human relationships depend upon four major concerns, and that the beginning and resolution of conflict is paralleled in the Scriptures.

1. If these four concerns are not handled successfully the group will be unproductive and tense, and group loyalty will be low. Persons come to a group with high personal needs and low group commitment. Close relationships are achieved when persons in the group have four needs met.

a) Groups can never feel like a "we" until each person gets his or her place in the group clear. The mixing and mingling of persons gives all participants a chance to model their skills, interests, and needs before one another. As the group observes, they mysteriously judge which person they want to provide what skill—encouraging that person and discouraging competitors. This obviously creates some tensions for persons who have limited skills, those who are timid, and those who are insistent about doing what they want and nothing else. The group tries to preserve each member whom they value, but the group will determine what each person is allowed to do. The group's needs determine the role each person plays; therefore, each person may perform a different role in another group.

Early conflict is usually over personal recognition: Who will do what? Where is each person important? Will the person and the group be satisfied with the arrangements made? How will the group deal with unmet needs? Deciding all these questions is hard work; and without some skills in relating and understanding, the group will fall apart, become disillusioned, or coldly reject the weaker, inexperienced persons. It is an emotional experience for most of us, since we must make ourselves open and vulnerable to the group's judgment if we are to be a part of the group. High personal self-esteem is needed for this task.

b) The second group issue is getting the purpose of the group clear. Everyone has certain wants and expectations, naïvely assuming that his or her needs are the same as those of others and that these needs are going to be met. Curious persons come to see, but are cautious because of past painful experiences. Individuals have needs; so do groups. Everyone, in fact, has different desires, and these desires keep changing. Groups must have leaders skilled in getting and keeping goals clear. Deep loyalties will not be formed until there is a common conviction about goals. Pluralism is destructive unless there is a common goal. A group whose members hold contradictory desires will be immobilized until they find a way to resolve their differences. Groups without clear goals face confusion, conflict, and frustration. (Non-profit groups often have fuzzy goals.) We demonstrate our poor skills when we avoid making clear goals. Our goals and beliefs govern our behavior. We have little choice but to learn to handle our conflicts and clarify our purposes, mission, and goals. Unclear goals guarantee feelings of failure and generate more emotion than handling the conflict responsibly.

Fortunately, we humans have a deep and powerful need for relationships, which lures us into making clear goals and generating commitment. Why should anyone want to go with us if we don't know where we are going? Common goals help us overcome many feelings of isolation, aloneness, and emotional discomfort.

c) The third concern we discovered at Mt. Sequoyah is that everyone needs an opportunity to have some say in the group. If you cannot influence your group—or your marriage—you soon become hostile, feel unimportant, and want to drop out. Most of us want to know how decisions are made in case we have a complaint. We are suspicious of dictators, tyrants, and insensitive people—people without "ears." We all yearn for freedom and for skills in influencing. Some try temper tantrums, others pout. Some use guilt, others intimidate. Each effort is a cry to be heard. Wise management of conflict must include clear and disciplined procedures by which each person can affect the quality of group relationships and group direction.

d) The fourth issue in the development of group relationships is the need to be loved. Not everyone wants the same level of closeness, so each person in the group must work out a satisfactory balance. Some persons want a deep, abiding, absolute loyalty, while others want a free come-and-go kind of relationship. Every church, group, or organization must help persons resolve this issue. Failure to cope with the need for closeness produces coldness, hurt feelings, and dropouts. No one can feel rejected without experiencing strong emotions.

Failure to deal with these four issues will kill group effectiveness, block group unity, create misunderstanding, generate emotional trauma, and leave us unable to live in peace.

2. The second learning in our Mt. Sequoyah conflicts was theological. Seminary had given me a lot of insights about human beings, but at Mt. Sequoyah we tested these insights by personal experience. We saw reenacted before our eyes the biblical drama of paradise, the fall, forgiveness, reconciliation, and struggle. Out of these observations came the conviction that the gospel is essential for peace in the world. The drama of successful conflict management we described in four acts. They are paralleled in the Scriptures:

a) Relationships often begin as idyllic paradise. Christians believe that they are created by God, made in God's image, and good! Genesis dramatically presents God's original design: harmony with God, self, others, and the world. God is in charge; humans have a prominent role in management, but they have clear restrictions, too. The opening drama is peaceful, hopeful, idyllic. We keep looking for that paradise—in groups, in vacations, in marriage.

b) The second act in our human drama is life's mess. People get overzealous about their own importance, make decisions without regard for God or others, lord it over others, and exercise self-serving aggressiveness. We experience the mess, see it in movies, and read of it in sacred and secular history. When persons disregard the restraints in life, and retain the winner-take-all philosophy, the paradise is wrecked, persons are hurt, angers grow strong, fears and guilts mount, and group life collapses. Dr. Hugh Halverstadt calls this "imperialistic humanity." Without the gospel, without repentance and forgiveness, the whole has no hope—the law of tooth and fang will prevail.

c) The third act of the drama is seen in Jesus Christ, who became God's means to restore community. The Bible tells us that God has intervened, and does intervene, to transform our mess to the original harmony. He acts to prevent our destructiveness, to lavish his mercy, and to restrain our human "imperialism." He calls for us to change, offers us forgiveness, and reestablishes the fourfold harmonious relationships we need: with God, others, self, and our environment. This work of God began in Abraham and is climaxed in Jesus, who created the church to witness and demonstrate the new life. At Mt. Sequoyah, groups who were able to acknowledge their destructive qualities were thrown into pangs of guilt, but when they saw their "sin"—imperialism—they could change, find forgiveness, and regain harmony.

d) The fourth experience in the drama of conflict is continued struggle. If we imagine some easy, magical, idyllic paradise, we multiply the problems with our denial of reality. The reality of life is struggle. After forgiveness, we still fail, hurt one another, and experience conflict. Imperialism remains in us. Twenty-three New Testament books tell about the struggle that Jesus' followers had maintaining Christian community. The struggle continues all of our lives. The balance between dominating others and sharing is hard to maintain. The gospel calls for us to grow from the darkness of absolute self-determination to the kingdom of God seen in the faith and love of Jesus Christ. We are only beginning to understand the skills of balance and harmony.

These theological insights demonstrate how essential the gospel is in healing the fractures in our relationships. We sense our capacity for and interest in destroying others who appear as enemies, and we assume they have the same thoughts about us. Without the drama of repentance, forgiveness, committed restraint, and continued struggle, our own attitudes will make us cynical and hopeless.

The gospel offers hope for the world. In place of the "might makes right" view, it encourages the restraint of love. It is not a fatalistic view telling us to adjust to the horrors of evil; it offers us mercy and the power to change. We don't have to settle for things as they are; we can work and dream of a world where God will help us use our conflict constructively, and we can see God's goodness.

I again observed these group needs, and my theological insights were enlarged, when a powerful group sought to take over the church, and when I moved to a large, historic, downtown church in a culturally diverse state.

Sometimes creating conflict is an act of love. I learned that when a powerful group sought to take over the minister's role in one church. When I discovered the plot, I had to decide whether to keep quiet or speak out and create a dreaded church fight. In this heated experience I learned the importance of the institutional church. While the institution hurts people sometimes, it has the power to reduce the destructiveness of human beings through formal procedures and restraints. Each church has procedures by which conflicts are handled. These procedures can be used as acts of love, guaranteeing fair play to all, and channeling the group's energy toward constructive purposes. Failure to organize allows for anarchy. Organizations can be evil, but they are also human vehicles by which human and theological values can be openly pursued. Intense conflicts must be handled by strong formal structures, or many people will be destroyed.

My next experience with conflict came when I was serving in a large church where power was strong and conflict was an everyday event. I sought in the gospel for the means of coping with the stress of constant conflict. Stress is created when a person seeks to preserve important values that are being threatened. Sometimes we want contradictory things and must choose. People blame us for things we deserve to be blamed for and for things we don't. The strongest ego is threatened without theological help.

From the Scriptures and from experience, I now believe that conflict is God's gift. Given this messed up world, we search for infallible guidance; yet where can it be found? Surely, every person is fallible. Can God be exhaustively described with twenty-six letters and forty-three sounds in English? Methodists say no. Rather, we believe the Holy Spirit, through living pastors, teachers, and laity in "conference," can be trusted to guide us into all truth. The tensions in life help us avoid heresy—carrying a good idea too far. Conflict helps us maintain the balance.

In coping with the stress, it helps to have a "grace-filled" friend who will help us shed the emotional garbage surrounding our conflicts. This person is God's "priest" to us, providing healing.

Sometimes conflict demands keeping people apart lest they destroy each other. At other times it means building bridges for relationships. Sometimes persons involved in conflicts need a referee who can provide rules of fair play to reduce the danger of our destructiveness getting out of control.

Conflict cannot be avoided. Jesus' disciples are called to manage conflict. He mastered the way, so that we have the theology to overcome conflict. Our world cries for help.

A small boy asked a world traveler if everyone could live in Texas. The traveler replied, "No, not unless they learned to live together." The most pressing agenda for our world is finding the skills, using our theological insights, and designing the loving structures by which we may live in peace. Now is the time to apply the good news of God's love in our daily living. It has been the means of saving the world before, and it offers us hope for our generation.